THE BEACH TEACHER

The Beach Teacher

Scriptural Lessons from the Shore

ALEXANDER J. BASILE

ST PAULS

Library of Congress Cataloging-in-Publication Data

Basile, Alex.
   The beach teacher: spiritual lessons from the shore / by Alexander J. Basile.
     pages cm
   ISBN 978-0-8189-1383-9
   1. Water in the Bible. 2. Water–Religious aspects–Christianity. I. Title.
   BS680.W26B37 2015
   242'.68–dc23
                                   2015004302

Produced and designed in the United States of America by the
Fathers and Brothers of the Society of St. Paul,
2187 Victory Boulevard, Staten Island, New York 10314-6603
as part of their communications apostolate.

ISBN 978-0-8189-1383-9

Current Printing - first digit   1   2   3   4   5   6   7   8   9   1 0

Place of Publication:
2187 Victory Blvd., Staten Island, NY 10314 - USA

Year of Current Printing - first year shown

2015   2016   2017   2018   2019   2020   2021   2022   2023   2024

Table of Contents

Acknowledgments

Special thanks to Tom Huggard for editing,
your guidance and lending your talent to my work.

To Father Thomas Cardone
for your friendship and mentoring.
Each project is special because of the gifts that you have given me.

To Allison, Alex and Maggie
every day at the beach is magical because of your love and laughter.

I dedicate this book to all those here
and in heaven who taught me a love for the shore!

Preface

Once the teacher, always a teacher! As you begin these reflections from the shore, Alex continues to demonstrate that God can be found wherever we go, all we have to do is stop, look and listen. It almost sounds as simple as the words in a first grade reader. However, in our fast paced culture, these words are essential if we are to grow in our interior lives as Christians.

Some days ago I was involved in a conversation where one of the speakers asked an individual, "Aren't you going to worry about what people will think?" The individual responded with a strong, "No, because most people do not think!"

Sometimes we can go through life by reacting but not thinking. This hurts not only our selves but also our relationships.

In *The Beach Teacher*, Alex invites us to stop and reflect about some essential elements in our lives. In a world where we tend to define ourselves by doing or by what we have or by efficiency, there will always be a personal emptiness. We need to be filled. This can only occur when we refocus on our being. Who we are in the innermost part of ourselves is known to God alone. Founder of the Marianists, Blessed William Joseph Chaminade said that "the essential is the interior." Where do you go to foster the interior? For Alex, it is the beach. But wherever you go, one must go somewhere to cultivate the mind and heart.

Water is a powerful symbol in our faith. Water speaks. As Alex relaxes in his beach chair on the shore he listens and sees the water. Water can be peaceful and calm. Water can be terrifying and damaging. Water can look fine on the outside, but deep below within there are tough currents. Life has all these dimensions and the Lord wants us to think about our spiritual lives from these perspectives.

Some of the themes that I found most helpful include the following:

The importance of healthy leisure as a support to the spiritual life.
Taking time to cultivate a spiritual imagination.
When God enters our lives, he wants everything.
The damage of gossip and the dealing with negativity.
Struggling with the deep roots of sin.
Mary receives grace without being afraid;
    do we resist or accept grace?
Surrender control and embrace trust.

I often ask my students, "When you think about the future, do you ever say to yourself, one day I want to grow up and be mediocre?" The answer is usually, "No, we want to be successful." This is the typical cultural answer. However, did you ever think that many Christians often choose mediocrity when it comes to a relationship with God? Alex challenges the reader to set aside mediocrity and embrace the challenges that come from having a dynamic relationship with God. He wants the reader to think, reflect and meditate. May we accept this challenge?

"May the Father and the Son and the Holy Spirit be glorified in all places to the Immaculate Virgin Mary!" (Marianist Doxology)

Father Thomas A. Cardone, SM
December 22, 2014

Introduction

Each summer, many people flock to the seashore to escape the oppressive heat. The cool breezes off the ocean or lake provide welcome relief from the stagnant humidity and rising temperatures. During the depths of winter, some seek the comfort of the beach to provide respite from the wicked chill.

If you picked up this book, I assume that you are one of the millions of people who enjoy the beach. Occasionally, you encounter individuals who will avoid the beach at all costs. Perhaps a fair complexion requires you to refrain from any extended exposure to the sun. I have a friend who considers sitting in the sand to be a similar experience as putting your feet in an ashtray. In a world where "one man's ceiling is another man's floor," spending time at the seashore may not be for everyone.

I am one of those people who love the beach. Annually, my grandparents rented a bungalow in Rockaway Beach, New York. They joined the thousands of other Irish immigrants who withdrew from the Bronx, Brooklyn and Manhattan to enjoy the refreshing breezes of the seashore. The "Irish Riviera," as it was known, did more than provide a place to vacation each year. The Rockaways became a home away from home. Irish music poured out of the dance halls as well as the cramped bungalows. Not only were souls refreshed, but friendships were also created and renewed each year in the fresh sea air.

My grandparents had five daughters and all of them joined their parents in renting bungalows in Rockaway Beach. The six umbrellas in the sand marked our territory on Beach 111th Street. Swimming, games of running bases, Frisbee and baseball soon gave way to a serious game of Whist (an Irish card game similar to Bridge) played by the adults and occasionally shared with us children. We only left the ocean long enough to grab a quick bite to eat. Thankfully, this temporarily allowed the adults to relinquish their roles as lifeguards. After the long day of out-door activity, our weary heads sank deep into our pillows until we woke to another day of fun in the sun.

As a teacher of religion, I remind my students to remain faithful to prayer and church attendance during the summer months. We can easily become distracted by the endless activities and change of routine during the summer months. For some people, the tranquility of the beach replaces the solemn atmosphere of church. The goal of this book is to affirm the importance of making our time at the beach or lake a Christ-centered experience while maintaining our connection to active worship.

While "imprisoned" in the classroom on beautiful days, my students beg me to take our class outdoors. After seventeen years of teaching, I have not yet relented to their frequent requests. *The Beach Teacher* flows from my constant yearning to emulate Jesus and place my students in the perfect outdoor setting. Most of what you will read in the following pages was written with my feet in the sand and with the sound of the crashing waves in the background. Many people around me have commented on my diligence while on vacation. But there is no need for pity. This book is a pure labor of love. I could think of no other place than the beach to construct my lessons in this book.

The average believer can easily become complacent as a part-time Christian. However, our association with Jesus requires us to infuse every day with His presence. The simple acts of going to work, school or while at leisure should include His teachings and perfect example.

The idea of writing a Christian book about the beach arose because Jesus spent many days of His ministry on the shores of the Sea of Galilee. The first disciples were plucked from their boats on the lake and called to become "fishers of men." The Scriptures depict our Lord preaching on the seashore on several occasions. Jesus utilized the cooler climate away from the city because He needed a break from the relentless heat. He also used this respite to preach to the flocks of people who would gather there.

Jesus resided often in Capernaum. This seaside town is often considered to be His second home. We are told that Jesus went to Capernaum immediately after He performed His first miracle in Cana. It seems that Peter and Andrew had also lived in this particular fishing village.

One of the most memorable appearances of Jesus on the beach occurs after the Resurrection:

> After this, Jesus revealed himself again to the disciples
> by the sea of Tiberias and he revealed himself in this
> way. Simon Peter, Thomas called the "twin," Nathan-

iel of Cana in Galilee, the sons of Zebedee and two others of his disciples were together. Simon Peter said to them, "I am going fishing." They said to him, "We will go with you." They went out and got into the boat, but that night they caught nothing. Just as the day was breaking, Jesus appeared on the beach, yet the disciples did not know it was Jesus.

(John 21:1-4)

There are often times that Jesus stands in our midst and we fail to recognize Him. Preoccupation with the daily grind forces us to overlook what should be the main focus of our lives. People head to the beach to relax and eliminate the stress caused by the frenzied pace of living in the modern age. We, unfortunately, eliminate what could become the greatest source of solace and tranquility. You should use Christ as the inspiration for meditation while at the beach or at the lake. When Jesus felt the pressure from the pressing crowds, He would retreat to quieter locations to regroup. We, too, must step away from the chaos and place ourselves in His presence.

The meditations in the following pages emerge from my summer sanctuary. Each chapter is meant to bridge our time at the shore to our faith lives. As you read this book, contemplate how you can walk in the footsteps of the greatest Teacher of all. May our reflections in the water be a reflection of the Perfect One. Use your time at the shore to rejuvenate your body, mind and soul.

Beach property always sells at a premium price. Wherever you travel, spending time at the shore is always expensive. The

Introduction

rich and famous have chosen the French and Italian Rivieras, Costa del Sol, Hawaii and the Caribbean as the prime places to frolic. Your time at the shore will appreciate all the more if you bring Christ with you on the journey. As you pack the beach bag, the cooler, the umbrella and chairs reflect on how your time at the water can help you boost your relationship with the head lifeguard, Jesus. He will be the one who will help you stay afloat in the roughest waters. Drowning in a world of fear, loneliness and chaos is a certain possibility without Jesus by your side. Rely on Him for safety and guidance. Make your beach your chapel away from your church.

Sitting with Our Lord at the Shore

1. Healthy leisure is essential for Gospel living. Spiritual tranquility is a must. What are you looking for at the shore? Do you have any spiritual goals?
2. Reflect on the past. What are your favorite memories of the beach or lake?
3. Picture Jesus with you at the beach. Simply use your imagination. Listen and be present to the moment.

THE BEACH TEACHER

1

The Joyful One

By the late 1970s, most of the bungalows in Rockaway Beach, New York were gone. The lack of summer tourism, the disrepair of the older bungalows and the hope of other building projects caused many of the summer cottages to be torn down. However, a few blocks of bungalows remained. Along with our relatives, our family rented a bungalow on Beach 108th Street. Each court or group of bungalows housed several two-bedroom cottages. My family rented a bungalow in the same court as my uncle who amazingly managed to fit himself and his eight children in his tiny bungalow. Families usually rented their traditional bungalow year after year.

Dorothy, a middle-aged widow, rented a bungalow diagonally across from ours. Dorothy loved to sing. Every morning as she cleaned her bungalow, Dorothy would unknowingly serenade the members of our close-knit summer community. Dorothy's performance would reach its crescendo when her favorite song on the radio, "Love Will Keep Us Together" played. Dorothy raised the volume of her stereo and battled The Captain and

Tennille for ownership of the song. My sister and I would sit on our porch and soak in Dorothy's enthusiastic performance. Other people in our court would smile in response. Her joy was unavoidable. Without realizing it, Dorothy brought a smile to others. Dorothy's morning sessions demonstrate the infectious nature of joy.

If you take a moment to recognize those people in your life who possess true joy, think about the characteristics that help this person or people to exude happiness. We all know a person who lights up the room upon entering it. They seem to possess "it." The "it factor" transcends money, power and fame. These people appear to capture the essence of what it means to be fully alive. Their magnetic personalities constantly attract others to them.

Real joy cannot be faked. It is a quality that permeates our being. It is not a temporary condition. It demands that we go beyond simply living in the moment. Our culture constantly anticipates the next holiday. We savor these high points in the year as an escape from the drudgery of everyday living. The indulgence in these days provides only momentary bliss. A genuinely joyful person does not need the boost of a holiday to maintain their upbeat attitude.

Joy propels an individual to do extraordinary things. The joyful attitude lifts an individual above the mundane. It assists us in transcending the place where most people blissfully remain content with the ordinary. As Thomas Jefferson stated, "Nothing can stop the man with the right mental attitude from achieving his goal; nothing on earth can help the man with the wrong mental attitude."

Since real joyfulness is an attitude and not a fleeting emotion, the individual can control this attitude. Only the individual will determine whether or not they will be happy. A student at Kellenberg Memorial once reminded me, "Happiness is an inside job!" Our friends may leave us and our fortune may be lost, but only we can choose how we will respond to a particular situation.

Those who possess real joy view life from a positive perspective. He or she is able to see possibilities when the outlook is bleakest. Humans tend to imagine the worst-case scenario. We are attracted to the gloom and doom that the media sells us. The evening news displays the latest horror in order to boost ratings. The more morbid the image, the harder it is to avert our eyes. We soon begin to believe that disaster will happen at any moment. Author and pastor Norman Vincent Peale gained fame as a motivational speaker and preacher on the power of positive living. Peale stated:

> Become a possibilitarian. No matter how dark things seem to be or actually are, raise your sights and see possibilities – always see them, for they're always there.

Believing that the best is possible is far easier with God. Peale incorporated a relationship with Christ into his message. Without Jesus, life is incomplete.

When people insist that you can be happy without believing in God, I always respond, "Show me a happy atheist and I will show you a person who is delusional to what the purpose of this life is all about." Everything in this life points clearly to a higher purpose. A Christ-centered existence demonstrates that everything in this life is of consequence. It is not a haphazard series of events. A joyful existence captures the hope of life eternal. Even in the midst of suffering, we discover exultation in our communion with Jesus Christ.

Christianity is more than a system of beliefs; it is placing our hearts and souls in the hands of the Son of God. He has a plan for us. This requires shedding our earthly wishes in exchange for the celestial. We often ignore this challenge because of the daily distractions that feed our selfish desires. The individual believes that he or she knows what is best for him or her. The reward for subscribing to God's plan is eternal joy. Bypassing a life in Christ results in missing out on the gift of joy both now and in heaven.

C.S. Lewis spoke about our inclination to ignore the invitation to eternal joy in exchange for immediate gratification. Humans relent far too easily to this temptation:

> If there lurks in most modern minds the notion that to desire our own good and earnestly to hope for the enjoyment of it is a bad thing, I submit that this notion has crept in from Kant and the Stoics and is no part of the Christian faith. Indeed, if we consider the unblushing promises of reward and the staggering nature of the rewards promised in the Gospels, it would seem that Our Lord finds our desires not too strong, but too weak. We are half-hearted creatures, fooling about with drink and sex and ambition when infinite joy is offered us, like an ignorant child

who wants to go on making mud pies in a slum because he cannot imagine what is meant by the offer
of a holiday at the sea. We are far too easily pleased.

(C.S. Lewis, *Into the Wardrobe*)

True joy also requires self-contentment. The internal critic
that resides within us is often our harshest judge. We avoid looking into the mirror for fear of what we will see. We magnify the
smallest blemish and dwell on the tiniest imperfections. We will
never be happy if we cannot accept ourselves as we are. When
you stop to examine the real you, be gentle. Dwell on the gifts
that you bring to the world rather than the superficial flaws.

Joy requires us to share it with others. Like Dorothy's morning serenade, we must let it out so that it may consume others.
Writer Mark Twain urged, "To get the full value of joy you must
have someone to divide it with."

As you face each day, count your blessings. A student who
was recently diagnosed with a brain tumor reassured her friends
who gathered by her hospital bed: "I am too blessed to be
stressed!" We can learn the secret to happiness by looking to the
joyful souls that surround us. Joy must be worn like an old comfortable jacket. Put it on and feel the warmth of joy. Show the
gloomy world how real happiness looks. Give them a glimpse
of how a life immersed in Christ transforms misery into elation.
Infuse the cloudy days with the blazing sun of summer. Embrace
each day as the excited child who runs with anticipation towards
the ocean. Dive into life and be the joyful soul!

We will turn to Blessed Mother Teresa for an explanation
of joy. May her inspirational words articulate the gift of joy in
our lives:

Joy is prayer – Joy is strength – Joy is love – Joy is a net of love by which you can catch souls. God loves a cheerful giver. She gives most who gives with joy. The best way to show our gratitude to God and the people is to accept everything with joy. A joyful heart is the inevitable result of a heart burning with love. Never let anything so fill you with sorrow as to make you forget the joy of the Christ risen.

(Mother Teresa)

Sitting with Our Lord at the Shore

1. Joy is a choice. Do you consider yourself a joyful person? What in your life has helped you to choose the attitude of joy?
2. Dorothy sang and for me that made a great difference. Who is a person in your life like Dorothy that possesses great joy? Why?
3. Life is a challenge and can in your own eyes demand from you more than you are willing to give. Your joy can turn sour. What are some of your personality patterns that prevent you from being joyful?
4. For Mother Teresa, joy and faith go hand in hand. Does your faith assist you in being a joyful person? Why?
5. Saint Thomas Aquinas said, "Joy is the noblest human act." What are the ways in which you bring joy to others?

2

Brotherly Correction

One of the standards of beach etiquette demands that you do not infringe upon another individual's or group's personal space. This includes: leaving enough room between yourself and others, keeping the volume of radio at a reasonable level, avoiding vulgarity and keeping a watchful eye on your children. Breaking these simple and what seem to be common sense rules can be the cause of a miserable day at the beach.

Recently, the tranquility of the beach was shattered by the screams of a young boy insisting that he would not listen to the guidance of his older sister. "I'm not going to do what you say, I don't care if mom said that you are in charge!" He barked loudly. The more mature sister attempted to reason with her brother, but to no avail. The one-sided screaming match seemed to last forever. Suddenly, a man sitting near the children gently rose from his beach chair and approached the unreasonable youth. The man knelt down on one knee, looked the boy in the eye and quietly explained how he should correct his attitude and behavior. Immediately, the boy changed his demeanor and calmly retreated to the shade of his umbrella. The man's kind and very direct approach immediately transformed what could have become a very uncomfortable situation.

There are many ways that people respond to the person whose behavior has gone awry. Rather than address the situation, some people attempt to discuss what has occurred with people outside of the actual event. Cell phones buzz with excitement as we gladly relate the miscues of a neighbor, coworker, classmate or relative. The stories begin to breathe on their own. Harmful gossip enables each hearer to interpret the tale and embellish it the way that he or she pleases. Detraction has seemingly more boundaries than gossip. It permits us to spread the reputation-damaging truth without any consideration for the harm that it may cause.

Keeping a scandalous story quiet would certainly benefit the wrongdoer. But silence or denial do not solve the problem either. We seldom consider the motivation behind our revealing the faults of others. Gossip and detraction distract us from concentrating on the problems that plague our own existence. Monotony seems to vanish momentarily as we fixate on the fascinating and even dysfunctional events of the day. We are silently relieved the trouble has bypassed us and chosen to reside in someone else's world for a change.

Jesus was accustomed to this harmful banter especially coming from a small town like Nazareth. Rumors spread like weeds along the dusty roads. He heard the murmuring by the well and the whispers in the market. He understood what it meant when a person looked around the room before they started speaking. The day the religious leaders brought the adulterous woman before Him, He pondered the sins of the accusers because they failed to recognize their own faults. Jesus looked into the dirt at His feet and began to write on the ground. Perhaps, He scribbled the sins of those armed with stones. Whatever the Teacher did on that day, He made the scribes and the Pharisees rethink their violent approach in attempting to alter the behavior of others.

Because Jesus knew our tendency to move in the wrong direction upon seeing or hearing that another person had made a mistake, He spoke directly about brotherly correction in the Gospels.

> If your brother sins against you go and tell him his fault between you and him alone. If he listens to you, you have won over your brother. If he does not listen, take one or two others along with you, so that every fact may be established on the testimony of two or three witnesses. If he refuses to listen to them, tell the Church. If he refuses to listen even to the Church, then treat him as you would a Gentile or a tax collector. Amen, I say to you, whatever you bind on earth shall be bound in heaven, and whatever you loose on earth shall be loosed in heaven. Again, I say to you, if two of you agree on earth about anything for which they are to pray, it shall be granted to them by my heavenly Father. For where two or three are gathered together in my name, there am I in the midst of them.   (Matthew 18:15-25)

The apostles would need to practice brotherly correction as much as anyone else. Jesus recognized how self-righteousness consumed the religious elite in Jerusalem. He hoped to avert the same condition for the chosen leaders in His new Church. In their new roles, these men would be asked to counsel the flock and comfort the troubled. Religious leaders are always aware of the missteps of the faithful because religion should initiate conversion. If they did not follow the proper techniques in pastoral leadership, unity would be lost within the community. If the apostles did not practice brotherly correction, how could the members of the early Christian communities be expected to do the same?

Resisting gossip is difficult. We nearly explode until we can relate the latest news with friends and family. As receivers of the rumors, we pump the storytellers for as much information as possible. Curiosity causes us to open the doors that are better left closed. Once a door is open, the toxic rumors last forever even without our assistance. We must remember this before we unleash harmful words against another.

Denial prevents us from recognizing our own defects. The outsider has a much better view of our talents and especially our faults. Proper communication is necessary in initiating this process. In His teaching on brotherly correction, Jesus provided some necessary guidelines for positive human interaction. The first principle that Jesus set forth is discretion. Instead of feeding our egos by garnering attention from others by revealing rumors or harmful stories about another, Jesus directs us to the person in need. When a person's life begins to spin out of control we only exasperate the situation by placing it in the public forum. Instead, Jesus wants us to provide personal attention. A kind word of encouragement, a gesture of compassion or straightforward guidance may be the remedy for a wayward soul. Jesus assisted many people in reconciling their problems without the public being aware of what He had said or done.

Brotherly correction must include charity. Love insists that we consider the well-being of the person involved in the error. We assist the sinner because we understand that overcoming the sin helps him to move closer to communion with God and others. True Christian charity requires us to know our role in resolving the problems of our brothers and sisters. Humility is an essential element of this role. We may tend to assume that we are better than the person we assist, but humility does not allow this to occur. It makes us conscious that we can easily end up in the same situation at any moment. Consider the feelings of the person you are helping. Listening to our faults is never easy. We must meditate on how we would react hearing the same thing about ourselves before dishing out the bad news.

Alerting others in the community to the faults of another simply helps us to reinforce the truth. However, we should take care to not form a jury willing to convict the person of a crime. Those enlisted to help must also remain faithful to the objective of the mission – to help another to correct harmful behavior. These people must share in the responsibility of acting as the hand of Christ, which will pull the sinner from the abyss.

The person we help may have sinned against us or other people we love. Without forgiveness, brotherly correction can never occur. Leave resentment outside of the situation. Healing cannot begin unless we move beyond the faults of the sinner and provide an avenue for reconciliation. An open heart to forgive may inspire the person we assist to be willing to face conversion.

Brotherly correction demands that the person offering advice reflect inward to make sure that he or she is not committing the same errors as the person they counsel. Many individuals have mastered the art of outward observation, but are blind when it comes to personal judgment. Use your role as a counselor to become a better person. The path to holiness begins with the recognition of our own misgivings.

There will be many opportunities to help others return to their place on the road to heaven. We have witnessed that even on a crowded beach, a Christ-like approach can be used. Be that gentle hand when a friend or loved one goes astray. Put them back on the path to righteousness. In the quiet moment at the shore reflect on how you can help others and at the same time improve the person within to live as Jesus Himself did. May this prayer by Saint Augustine remind us of the importance of self-abandonment while at the same time attempting to perfect self-knowledge especially when others are in need. For once we understand ourselves we can truly help others.

> Lord Jesus,
> Let me know myself and know Thee,
>   and desire nothing save only Thee.
> Let me hate myself and love Thee.
> Let me do everything for the sake of Thee.
> Let me humble myself and exalt Thee.
> Let me think nothing except Thee.
> Let me die to myself and live in Thee.
> Let me accept whatever happens as from Thee.
> Let me banish self and follow Thee,
>   and ever desire to follow Thee.

Let me fly from myself and take refuge in Thee,
   that I may deserve to be defended by Thee.
Let me fear for myself, let me fear Thee;
   and let me be among those who are chosen by Thee.
Let me distrust myself and put my trust in Thee.
Let me be willing to obey for the sake of Thee.
Let me cling to nothing save only to Thee,
   and let me be poor because of Thee.
Look upon me, that I may love Thee.
Call me that I may see Thee and forever enjoy Thee.

Sitting with Our Lord at the Shore

1. We have all been in situations where we have seen another's negative behavior, a behavior that is harmful, hurtful, self-destructive or damaging to community. First, we make an internal judgment. Then what?
2. Relationships are complex. How do you deal with brotherly or sisterly correction? Or do you simply avoid it?
3. News spreads. Aided by social media, gossip has a new venue in life. Gossip is contagious. Where do you stand? Are you a gossip or a trusted individual known for compassion and advice?
4. A wise individual both seeks and is open to advice. How have others given you advice when you have made mistakes?

3

The Urge to Talk

Many years ago, an unusual beach tradition developed in the vicinity of Beach 111th Street in Rockaway Beach. The religious sisters who ran Stella Maris High School would ring the Angelus bell at 6 a.m., at noon and at 6 p.m. The ancient prayer calls the faithful to pause in the midst of the busy day and reflect on the angel Gabriel's Annunciation to the Blessed Virgin Mary. The prayer was brought to light beautifully by the painting of Jean-Francois Millet (as seen in the picture left). The *Angelus* hangs today in the Louvre, in Paris.

When the bells rang at noon and at six o'clock in the evening everyone on the beach stopped and faced the direction of the bells. Those seated would rise and do the same. The people aware of this local tradition participated in this practice daily. It did not seem to matter the faith denomination of the individual. For the person who did not understand the meaning of the Angelus, the moment of silence served as an opportunity to reflect on the transcendent and the Mind behind it all.

As a child, I did not know the actual Angelus prayer. But

the two interruptions to my beach day taught me a certain respect for prayer. My cousins and I were expected to stand at attention as a soldier does at inspection. Reflecting back on my experience in Rockaway, it was not as out of the ordinary as it may have seemed. If the beach is the perfect place for contemplation, why don't we use its tranquility to cultivate our prayer life?

The Angelus is a unique expression of faith as we publicly pause to reflect on our relationship with God. As Millet would portray in his famous painting, the farmers ceased work momentarily to infuse God into their day. With their feet still firmly planted in the soil, they united the heavenly with the earthly. God permeates even the mundane moments. Manual labor is given a higher purpose when fused with the divine. How well do you integrate your daily life with prayer?

In a task-oriented world, we may procrastinate when it comes to matters "unseen." God may not enter our thoughts as we trudge throughout our day. We may relegate prayer to Sunday. Even the Sabbath has been transformed in the nonstop world. The day which had been set apart to rest and worship our Creator is now as hectic as the other days of the week. If and when we enter church the interior clock is set to the secular world. We set our mental alarms to an hour and we become annoyed when Mass goes beyond the allotted time.

We forget that the main objective of our time in worship is to enter into communion and conversation with God. Prayer becomes an essential component of this experience. Prayer must flow from the individual. It is difficult to cram all that we want to say to God into one hour of the week. When life becomes a continual prayer, our communication with God never ceases.

The most menial tasks evolve into loving actions dedicated to reaching our ultimate potential within our relationship with our Father. There is less wasted motion. More of our life and daily activity has significance.

Prayer keeps things in perspective. Prayer refines a situation and prevents it from spinning out of control. It points us in a positive direction. It is a road map to God. Prayer assists us in focusing on our final destination. It is as vital as a pilot's radio transmission to air traffic control. We must continue communication until we have landed safely home.

We mistakenly believe that our prayers alter the mind and will of our Father in heaven. The actual purpose of prayer is to transform our own hearts and minds to conform to God's. Prayer opens the ears of the soul and allows it to listen to His commands. It will be through our obedience to the will of the Father that we will truly be transformed.

Prayer is the ultimate communication with God. When we desire to reveal the person hiding beneath the superficial shell, we sit and talk to him. The same is true with God. It is only through prayer that we can pierce the barrier of invisibility that exists between God and us. Some people attempt to discover God through academic study and become increasingly frustrated because it usually fails to yield any answers. Prayer provides a genuine glimpse into our Creator.

The Church preaches "lex orandi, lex credendi." The Latin is translated as the "law of prayer, is the law of belief." The Church teaches that prayer shapes our belief. We usually approach prayer in the opposite manner. The way we pray may unfortunately depend on how we feel at the moment. When we do not feel inspired, we can dismiss prayer. True spiritual growth occurs when we pray despite the dark nights of the soul and when apathy manifests itself. Prayer has the ability to enlighten the gloomy spirit and transport it to the light. This adage confirms the advice of my father: "When in doubt, pray."

Prayer serves as a bridge between the human and divine. People overlook the ability to experience the heavenly realm while still on earth. Sainthood does not occur by sheer coincidence or by withdrawing to the sidelines. Those involved in an active prayer life actively pursue the ultimate goal of a place in the kingdom of heaven. Saints are made by a commitment to conversion that is promoted through prayer.

Prayer serves as the catalyst for personal growth. It is fertilizer for the soul. If we are going to grow as Christians and in our relationship with God, we must pour ourselves into prayer. By praying continually, our intimacy with God transforms us.

Prayer is similar to sunblock protection against the harmful effects of sin. Sin can't penetrate the defensive layer that the constant conversation with God provides. With our hearts fixed upon heaven, we can repel the advances of our selfish desires.

The days at the beach or lake permit us to quietly contemplate our lives. Utilize this time well. Include some prayer in these moments of meditation. Open your heart and soul to Jesus. Call upon the saints for guidance. Put yourself in His presence and get to know Him better. Bridge the gap in your relationship with God.

Twenty years after I had stood on the shores of Rockaway Beach with my entire family, I finally learned the Angelus prayer. The simple and easily memorized prayer has become a staple in my life and at Kellenberg Memorial High School where I teach. Every day at twelve o'clock, the students of our school pause no matter where they are to pray. Students in the hallway, cafeteria and classroom stand or sit in place and reflect on God's call to a young girl in Nazareth. This practice is a wonderful example to pray no matter where we are or what we are doing. Use this prayer as inspiration of how our Blessed Mother surrendered herself to God the Father. As the clock strikes twelve and six, remember her words to the angel Gabriel.

> The Angel of the Lord declared to Mary:
> And she conceived of the Holy Spirit.
>
> Hail Mary, full of grace, the Lord is with thee;
> blessed art thou among women
> and blessed is the fruit of thy womb, Jesus.
> Holy Mary, Mother of God, pray for us sinners,
> now and at the hour of our death. Amen.
>
> Behold the handmaid of the Lord:
> Be it done unto me according to Thy word.
>
> Hail Mary...
>
> And the Word was made Flesh:
> And dwelt among us.
>
> Hail Mary...
>
> Pray for us, O Holy Mother of God,
> that we may be made worthy of the promises of Christ.
>
> Let us pray:

Pour forth, we beseech Thee, O Lord,
Thy grace into our hearts;
that we, to whom the incarnation of Christ, Thy Son,
was made known by the message of an angel,
may by His Passion and Cross be brought
to the glory of His Resurrection,
through the same Christ Our Lord. Amen.

Sitting with Our Lord at the Shore

1. Saint Paul urges us to "pray constantly" in order to grow in the way of Christ. This is a difficult challenge! How often do you pray? Is prayer an important element of your life?

2. Atmosphere can have a transforming effect in terms of where we pray. Certain places or areas can be more conducive for prayer. Do you ever pray at the beach? Where do you go to pray?

3. Jesus says, "Where two or more are gathered, I am there." Jesus encourages us to pray in communion or community. Do you ever pray with your spouse? Do you invite other members of your family or your friends to pray?

4. For me, the Angelus has contributed to my growth in prayer. What are the prayers that have transformed you? Do you rely on any particular scripture verses in times of peace or conflict?

4

The Wrong Way

In May of 2008, my family, including my parents, sister and brother-in-law and their three daughters ventured to Fort Lauderdale, Florida to take advantage of a long spring weekend. We arrived at the beach in the morning to get the most out of our first day. A few minutes after we had settled in, three college students placed their towels in the sand a few feet away from us. Immediately, one boy reached into his backpack and pulled out the funnel and hose. Instinctively, another boy immediately assumed his position, lying on his back at the bottom of the hose. The boy who held the funnel, cracked open a beer with his free hand and emptied the contents of the can into the funnel. The boy at the bottom of the hose sucked in the liquid from the hose. Each of the boys took their turn consuming a beer. They repeated the ritual about every ten minutes until the effects of the process rendered two of the three students unconscious.

This story unearths many disturbing trends that need to be discussed. Underage drinking, the binge culture and unsupervised minors are all subjects that could be addressed. But this snapshot of unhealthy beach life opens the door for much-needed discussion on the vices or tendencies that are harmful to us.

We are all creatures of habit. We are attracted to certain objects and particular behavioral patterns. As the owner of a delicatessen for over twelve years, customers were surprised when one of us behind the counter knew a person's order before they had spoken. We are creatures of comfort. Just as we choose the same few items at our favorite restaurant, we also settle into various patterns of behavior.

It is no surprise that the very first book of the Bible deals with the human struggle against sin. We assume that temptation is the greatest cause leading to sin. Temptation may dangle the carrot that makes us contemplate the sin, but it is our selfishness that seals the deal. Delving into sin causes an individual to prefer himself to others. Sin says, "I want what I want and I am not concerned about hurting myself or others!"

The most detrimental consequence of sin is not only the one time offense, but the endless cycle that it initiates. We have all heard someone beg forgiveness for a particular wrongdoing, but later on wonder why this same person is found guilty for that same sin time and time again. The habit of sin can easily consume a person. We often use the seven deadly sins to illustrate the pitfalls that humans must avoid in order to discover the moral life. These sins are listed as greed, lust, pride, envy, sloth, gluttony and anger. These sins serve as the root system for other sin. They are often referred to as the "seven deadly sins" because they provide the gateway that leads to more serious sin.

Selfishness may be perceived as serving the interest of an individual. But since selfishness is the opposite of self-love, it actually causes us severe harm. The constant focus on the individual will prevents one from seeing the virtuous and the good. Selfishness builds a wall between us and the ability to love.

If we concentrate on the meaning of each capital sin, we may be able to understand how they act as the foundation of other sins.

Pride as a capital sin goes beyond the healthy self-contentment of one's actions. Here, pride is defined as excessive preference of oneself over God and others. There is an intense desire to be noticed by others not because it is well deserved, but to quench a disordered self-esteem. Our desire to take our place on the top of the pyramid causes us to forget the value of God and others.

Envy prompts us to focus on what we are missing rather than what we have. We live in the inadequacy of misery. Feeling that we can never measure up to the good fortune of others, we knowingly and unknowingly rejoice in their misfortune and sorrow. Falling prey to envy leaves us even emptier than before as we allow this sin to penetrate our being.

Anger is a sin when it is more than a rise of emotions in reaction to injustice. Wrongful anger seeks revenge on others. It inspires harmful remuneration as vengeance. Sinful anger spawns hurtful words or actions well beyond the initial wrongdoing against us. The effects of anger may cause everlasting damage to our relationships and the reputations of others.

Lust causes the individual to have an inordinate desire for earthly pleasure. In the chapter "The Body Beautiful," we will discuss the manner in which lust dehumanizes another person in our search for sexual gratification. Lust tempts us to acquire earthly pleasure at any price even at the loss of our dignity and the dignity of others.

Greed (otherwise referred to as *avarice*) breeds an excessive attachment to material possessions and the riches of this world. When Jesus preached that His disciples should "fix their hearts on things above, rather than things of this earth," He was conscious of our tendency to love the things of this world. Humans often forget that our loftiest goal should reach well beyond the confines of Earth.

Sloth is the sin of inactivity. This type of laziness prevents us from fulfilling our obligations towards God and others. Apathy cultivates a realm of inertia in an individual. The "I don't care" and "I can't deal" attitudes paralyze us. Sloth urges us to push off our responsibilities to another time. Although everyone needs time to recharge his or her batteries, there is always a requirement to accomplish certain tasks.

Gluttony is the sin of overindulgence. As the young people at the beach demonstrate, we need to know our limitations. Gluttony usually concerns excessive eating and drinking; however, it is not limited only to food and drink. Too much of any activity can be destructive. Overindulgence may also occur when shopping, watching television, playing video or computer games, etc. The tendency to gluttony may also open up the pathway to addiction.

To combat poor behavior, it is vital to replace these habits with good, true and reasonable actions. The virtues assist us in using our free will properly. As defined in the *Catechism of the Catholic Church* (#1833), "the habitual and firm disposition to do good" (virtues) would contradict the capital sins with self-discipline, compassion, responsibility and honesty. The virtues make love possible by removing the pest of selfishness from our daily living.

The cardinal virtues (which is derived from "cardo" in Latin which means "hinge") are prudence, fortitude, justice and temperance. These habits literally unlock moral goodness. There is an amazing reciprocal quality to the virtues in that they reveal a fulfilling existence where we may serve God and others. By practicing virtuous behavior, each of these qualities within us is strengthened.

The theological virtues are faith, hope and love. Called "theological" because we believe that they are God-given, these virtues dispose humans to a deeper relationship with the Holy Trinity. We receive these gifts through the Sacrament of Baptism when we enter into our relationship with God. They continue to grow as we develop as Christians through participation in prayer, Mass, the Sacraments and virtuous living.

When you examine your daily patterns, which of the above habits described you? Are you more prone to vice or virtue? Bad habits are easier to adopt than good ones. In sin, we turn away from God. We reject the goodness He offers. Satan's proposal to accept sin can be initially far more attractive, because it provides immediate gratification. The Prince of Darkness is an excellent salesman. Beware of his diligence. Our society unknowingly endorses many of these sins as it attempts to promote its latest agenda.

The virtues require self-denial and discipline that our complacent self may find too difficult to adopt. We grow content by conforming to a life of mediocrity. Change can be painful especially when it calls for a dramatic modification of our normal behavior. The self-nurturing quality of the virtues continues to assist us once we begin to make them part of us.

These habits have far more impact on our lives than searching for our usual spot at the beach or eating our usual breakfast. These behavioral patterns have the ability to alter our eternal destination and improve our relationships immediately. Spend some time to reflect on your habits, good and bad. Contemplate whether your behavior is bringing you closer to Jesus or driving a wedge between you and others. Making Christ and others a priority will assist you in implementing the virtues into your life.

Once you are able to identify your sins, seek forgiveness for your misgivings. The love of Christ erases our transgressions and allows us to travel the road to reconciliation. Use the example of Saint Augustine who sought to transform his brokenness into a fulfilled existence. This notable saint's path to heaven was riddled with the potholes of sin. Eventually he discovered his worthiness through virtue. Turn your life in the right direction by embracing the virtues. We leave you with his plea:

> What fault committed by man has not been
> expiated by the Son of God made man?
> What pride can be so immeasurably inflated
> that it could not be brought down by such humility?
> Truly, O my God, if we were to weigh
> both the offenses committed by sinners,
> and the grace of God the Redeemer,
> we would find that the difference equaled
> not only the distance between east and west,
> but the distance between hell and the highest heaven.

O wonderful Creator of light,
by the terrible sorrows of Your Son,
pardon my sins!
Grant, O God, that His goodness
may overcome my wickedness,
that His meekness may atone for my perversity,
that His mildness may dominate my irascibility.
May His humility make amends for my pride;
His patience, for my impatience;
His benignity, for my harshness;
His obedience, for my disobedience;
His tranquility, for my anxiety;
His sweetness, for my bitterness;
may His charity blot out my cruelty!

(Saint Augustine)

Sitting with Our Lord at the Shore

1. Sin is universal to all; yet we all have our own particular struggles. What applies to one (impatience, envy, etc.) does not apply to all. Which sin is your greatest challenge?

2. Sin, like a tree, often has deep roots. Think to what degree is selfishness rooted within? Saint Thomas Aquinas says that we usually do not choose evil as evil but sugarcoat it as choosing good for me. How do you rationalize your sin and make it seem good?

3. Temptation has been around since Adam and Eve. How do you deal with it? Do you pray to avoid sin?

4. Thank God for second chances! How often do you receive the Sacrament of Reconciliation?

5

Motherly Love

When I was a child, my mother orchestrated the planning of our excursions to the beach. Even when my father had to work, she managed to transport our family to the beach with relative ease. Many mothers also partake in the endeavor of bringing their children to the beach. On a weekday, while many husbands work, mothers trudge through the soft sand with strollers laden with supplies for the day. What may seem to be too much effort for little reward occurs daily so that families can enjoy some well-deserved time at the shore.

This active motherly sacrifice is only one aspect of what mothers do for their loved ones. The unconditional love of mothers should spark a reflection on what we need to do for others. As we sit by the shore, we may want to ponder our relationship with not only our own mothers but also with Mary, the mother of Jesus.

We refer to the Blessed Mother as the "Mother of all" because of her role in Salvation History. Real love occurs when there is no hesitation in its giving. Mary willingly surrendered her

Son for the redemption of all humanity. Along with Christ, she suffers on our behalf. Jesus Christ's death on the cross provides a victory over sin for all. Just as no one is left behind where God's mercy is concerned, Mary's love for us does not discriminate either.

Jesus lived in obscurity in Nazareth for nearly thirty years. Because they are considered the "hidden years" of the Holy Family and in the life of Christ, we seldom give them much thought. They are literally "out of sight and out of mind." But these were important years of formation in the life of Jesus. His main teachers, Mary and Joseph, played a vital role in His life. One of the earliest stories in the Gospels centers on Simeon, the prophet, who was waiting in the Temple to see the Messiah. During these years in Nazareth, Mary had to live with the words of the prophet Simeon in her heart for the entire time. "A sword will pierce your heart" are not words that any mother wants to hear. Especially after angelic intervention, Mary understood that the earthly journey with her Son would not be a simple task. Mary prompted her Son to perform His first miracle at the marriage feast at Cana. This act would begin His public ministry and place Him on the road to His crucifixion. We may ask, "Why would she do such a thing?" The answer is simple: Mary knew the unconditional motherly love demanded that she not only take care of her Son but all of her children as well.

Looking at the actions of the "handmaid of the Lord" should awaken us to the important notion that our lives are not only about us. Mary's life as a witness demonstrates the fact that the more we give to others the more we can find fulfillment. Mary is love personified. She is created with love from the Father and bestows this love on their Son. In those ordinary days in Nazareth, Mary reinforced her lessons of flawless love.

The Blessed Mother illustrates the perfect pattern of hu man behavior. Very often, our choices revolve around our convenience. None of Mary's options would be placed under the category of convenience. Humans can't be blamed for seeking an easy solution to our problems. Every day is packed with struggles in life that seem to fight us at every turn. Mary demonstrates how our self-giving in the face of adversity can lead to eternal happiness and everlasting union with God.

Many Christians are content with a personal stash of faith, but hesitate to openly profess the Gospel. They fear being labeled a "Jesus freak," a person who is equated with the bell-ringing evangelist who lives in a spiritual fairyland. These are the people we avoid at parties, in school or at the office. We run the other way as they approach us. They seem utterly out of touch with reality.

Mary's persuasiveness at the wedding feast of Cana also reminds us to be willing to share Christ with the rest of the world. Life together in tranquil Nazareth made Mary very happy. But in Nazareth she would never experience the joy that she would discover by letting the world in on one of the most profound secrets. The gift of Christ must be something that we, too, are willing to share.

Mary unveils Jesus to us in a unique way. She allows Him to do all of the talking. The phrase "Do whatever He tells you," are the last words we hear our Mother speak in the Gospels. Most Christians assume that Mary utters some profound phrase at the crucifixion. Not so. Mary exemplifies that when we live and breathe Christ, no other words are necessary. Virtuous living and a clear connection to Christ will be all that we need to share His message with the world.

The Blessed Mother gives us guidance in helping us cope with our fears. When you ask a person to articulate their fears, he or she usually explains how they want to avoid a particular object or an action at all cost. We attempt to close the door on our fears and keep them as far away as possible. We prefer to place as much distance between our fears and ourselves or forget about them altogether.

At the Annunciation, Mary is confronted with God's plan by the angel Gabriel; the frightened girl confounds us with her openness: "Be it done unto me according to your word." In a defiant exclamation to her fears, the young woman's confidence in God outweighs any trepidation. Even as a young girl, she understands the power of her relationship with God. With the Almighty on her side, fears dissipate. Rather than run from her fears, Mary allows her faith in the Lord to crush them. With God all things are possible. Compared to the awesomeness of God, even the grandest fear is insignificant. The relationship with God can be the mightiest sword in the battle against our fears. Rely on heavenly bonds to assist you in overcoming your fears.

When suffering emerges some believers abandon their relationship with God. Mary chose the alternative path. The mother of Jesus opened a special place in her heart for her Heavenly Father who assisted her in making sense of the anguish that her Son had to endure. Many pieces of classical art portray Mary standing beside Jesus at the foot of the cross. She took on His suffering and sorrow. When the closest friends of her Son had run away and hid, Mary becomes a rock of faith. Mary faced her most challenging moment in a manner that should always be in our mind when suffering appears. Cling to your relationship with God when difficulty presents itself.

Sainthood requires that difficult choices must be made. Mary is an unusual saint. Most saints made the transformation from selfishness to complete selflessness. Saints were usually ordinary people who originally gave in to the temptations of life. They illustrate that the greatest challenge of life will be avoiding the self-centered nature of our desires. Mary, made perfect through the Immaculate Conception, continued to articulate her flawless nature throughout her earthly life until she entered heaven with her Assumption.

Mary's perfect earthly existence helped her to attain a unique status. Because she was sinless, Mary's body was assumed body and soul into heaven after her life had ended. The Feast of the Assumption is commemorated on August 15th. Some beach communities celebrate this feast by entering the ocean or lake three times for a special indulgence. In some cases there is a special blessing of the ocean and an occasion for the blessing of the sick.

Perhaps the best tribute to mothers is Marian devotion. Mothers can probably appreciate the Blessed Mother better than the rest of us. Mothers can sympathize with the endless worrying and sleepless nights. They know the importance of letting go so a child can learn from his or her own mistakes. Most of all, mothers know the dread that harm will come to their child. No matter who we are, we can all use the mother of Christ as the ultimate example.

"Stella Maris" is a popular nickname given to Mary. It literally means "Star of the Sea." Just as mariners would look to the stars to chart their course, the Blessed Mother can be our light in the darkness. She will provide guidance when we are having trouble finding our way. The world will do all it can to stand in the way of Christ. Mother Mary will show us the direct course to Jesus. Every time that you gaze out onto the water, contemplate the motherly example that you need to follow.

While thinking about all that our mothers have done for us, we must be sure to meditate on the role of Mary in the life of Jesus. Motherly intervention takes on a whole new meaning. Permit Mary to set *your* agenda. Use her peace and prayerfulness to help you plan your journey. When you are lost, she will lead you back to her Son. Mary is the key that unlocks our most precious treasure. Allow our Mother to give your vision a sharper focus on Jesus in your life.

Mary joined other heroic Biblical women with her song of praise for the intervention of the Lord in her life. Mary's version is called the *Magnificat*. Pray along with Mary as she thanks God for His grace and everlasting love.

My soul proclaims the greatness of the Lord;
my spirit rejoices in God my Savior.
For He has looked upon His handmaid's lowliness;
behold, from now on will all ages call me blessed.
The Mighty One has done great things for me,
and holy is His name.
His mercy is from age to age to those who fear Him.
He has shown might with His arm,

dispersed the arrogant of mind and heart.
He has thrown down the rulers from their thrones
but lifted up the lowly.
The hungry He has filled with good things;
the rich He has sent away empty.
He has helped Israel His servant,
remembering His mercy,
according to His promise to our fathers,
to Abraham and to his descendants forever.

Let her voice be one with yours in praising God for all the wonderful things that He has done for you.

Sitting with Our Lord at the Shore

1. Mary listens, understands and says "Yes" to God. Which quality of Mary touches your heart?
2. Mary received grace without being afraid. How open are you to God's grace?
3. God laughs at our plans. As with Mary, He takes us out of our comfort zones. All He requires is surrender and trust. Can you do as Mary did?
4. Mary stands at the foot of the cross as a suffering mother. In times of darkness, sadness or death do you approach her in prayer?
5. The Assumption of Mary reminds us that we too may share in the glory of heaven. Until then, whom do we rely on? Besides Mary, do you have a saint in heaven that you rely on to bring your prayers to our heavenly Father?

6

The Body Beautiful

Necessity being the mother of invention, when the women's Olympic rowing team needed a more practical and flexible outfit in the early 1900's, Carl Jantzen created a uniform for them. Although the outfit did not expose too much skin, controversy erupted when the rowing suit was deemed too tight and showing too much of the human form. However, Jantzen's invention sparked an interest in a more comfortable bathing suit for women. This began an evolution of the swimsuit that started to show more and more skin. Although revealing the navel was still taboo, once the stomach was exposed the design of the bathing suit changed dramatically.

In 1946, French designer, Jacques Heim advertised his new bathing suit along the French Riviera. Heim called his new suit the "Atome" (which was named after the atom which was recently discovered) because of the suit's small size. A few weeks later, another French designer, Louis Reard, upstaged Heim. Reard's "bikini" was named after Bikini Atoll where nuclear testing had occurred a few weeks before.

Reard had difficulty in finding a model to showcase his new controversial creation. Reard hired Micheline Bernardi. The model had no hesitation in showing her body in public because of her job as an exotic dancer in Paris. When the tiny suit premiered, it was immediately banned throughout Europe and many people in America thought the suit was far too scandalous for beaches.

Today, the bikini is considered appropriate apparel for the beach. It is also acceptable on many European beaches to go topless. But without being prudish, have we actually given any thought to why we appear at the beach in nothing more than our underwear? People certainly had this perception of the bikini in 1946. This would be the obvious reason why Louis Reard had to hire a stripper to model his beachwear. More than fifty years later we would not give this subject a second thought. Society has its way of deeming a trend "shocking" one minute and acceptable the next.

The beach has become a showcase of the body. Many people adopt the philosophy "less is more." Many use the shore as an opportunity to reveal tattoos and body piercings. Some individuals even exhibit religious images on his or her body as art. Tattoos of crosses appear in some unusual places. "Branding ourselves with Christ" has taken on an entirely new meaning and possibly without any spiritual impact on the individual bearing the art.

It is not surprising that these fashion trends have coincided with the increase of sexual promiscuity. I am grateful that our school employs a uniform requirement. A consistent wardrobe amongst students alleviates the pressure placed on parents and young people who are often forced to conform to the rest of society. Friends who teach in the public school system relate many stories of dealing with girls who come to school in inappropriate outfits. Many of these girls are uncomfortable wearing outfits that reveal far too much but choose to wear them because it is the norm to do so. Our inner desire to fit in and be accepted coerces us into following the herd.

Our culture has dangerously promoted a message to women that the more skin that is exposed, the more tantalized men will be. Dressing in a small bikini will no doubt garner more attention from the male world. Pop history has proven that Farrah Fawcett, Cheryl Tiegs, Christie Brinkley, Kathy Ireland, and Kate Upton received fame and fortune from swimsuit photos and posters. Some of these women became overnight sensations. Their faces became instantly recognizable.

The newest pinup girls quickly claim their places in pop iconography. Why? Lust. Sex sells. This may seem like a damning conviction of the male mind and soul. But let's face reality, the average man does not cruise the annual *Sports Illustrated* swimsuit edition to admire the intellectual advances of women. He does so to indulge in the "eye candy." Lust deteriorates what may seem as the admiration of women into empty calories that provides absolutely no nourishment to the body, mind and soul. Lust turns the person we "gaze upon" into a mere object. Lust removes our concern for the well-being for members of the opposite sex.

Lust affects both men and women. I have used the examples above because they are well documented. Men seem to be more blatant in their "navel gazing" than women. Women are certainly susceptible to the pitfalls of lust. Television shows and magazines target women with their "top ten" lists of the most beautiful man alive and provocative love stories. Lust is a sneaky entity and the people who use it to lure us are just as cagey.

The virtue of modesty is our greatest weapon in a world that uses the human body in a harmful manner. I often use the analogy of a Christmas or birthday present to explain modesty to my students. Imagine how a person would feel if he or she were handed an unwrapped gift. Most of us would certainly prefer that the present be covered in beautiful wrapping. Why do we wrap gifts? My students and I agree that the purpose of wrapping a present is to add to the surprise and to heighten the anticipation of discovering what lies underneath the wrapping. Humans are attracted to mystery. It is for this reason why so much of God remains unknown. He leaves us wanting for more. Much value stands within the expression and advice to "leave something to the imagination."

I do not want you to think that this chapter is a call for the return of Victorian or Puritan ideals. I am not promoting the wearing of burqas or full cover-ups at the beach. The goal of this chapter is to wake all of us to the nature of our desires and that these desires can easily degrade the human body. The body that God has given us is the tabernacle to the soul during our earthly existence.

Pope John Paul II quoted Saint Paul on the topic of modesty:

Saint Paul writes in the First Letter to the Thessalonians: "…this is the will of God, your sanctification:

that you abstain from unchastity, that each one of you know how to control his own body in holiness and honor, not in the passion of lust like heathens who do not know God." (1 Thessalonians 4:3-5)

After some verses, he continues: "God has not called us for uncleanness, but in holiness. Therefore whoever disregards this, disregards not man but God, who gives his Holy Spirit to you."

(Pope John Paul II, General
Audience of January 28, 1981)

The temple of the body houses the soul. How do we treat the beautiful tabernacle that God provides us during our earthly lives?

Men and women seem to be held to different standards. "Boys are allowed to be boys" while girls are expected to be proper and demure. Dr. Alice von Hildebrand dealt with the precious nature of the female body:

...there is something extraordinarily great and mysterious about femininity. And why do I say it is so great and so mysterious? Because you all know that every little girl that is born, is born with a seal, so to speak, protecting the mystery of her femininity which is the womb. There is a seal and if you understand, a seal always indicates something which is sacred. The seal, which doesn't exist in the male body, is profoundly symbolic and says this belongs to God in a special way.

Modern society dismisses sanctity of the female body in favor of the more provocative way it is presented. The masterminds behind this philosophy ignore the human capacity of mastery over our body and sexual desires. Rational and intelligent creatures rise above the instinctual behavior of animals. Humans have the capability to think before we act. At least we hope so. We possess the capability to defeat the temptation of lust and disrespect of the body.

Our gift of sharing in the co-creative power of God should override the mentality that treats the body as a mere object. Eliminate the unnecessary objectification of the body in your world. Encourage others to tune out the cultural stereotypes that cause us to be sucked into the temptations of the flesh. Saint Alphonsus Liguori, who understood that the Blessed Mother held the secret to chastity, composed the following prayer:

> Mary, Mother most pure, and Joseph, chaste guardian of the Virgin, to you I entrust the purity of my soul and body. I beg you to plead with God for me that I may never, for the remainder of my life, soil my soul by any sin of impurity. I earnestly wish to be pure in thought, word and deed in imitation of your own holy purity. Obtain for me a deep sense of modesty, which will be reflected in my external conduct. Protect my eyes, the windows of my soul, from anything that might dim the luster of a heart that must mirror only Christ-like purity. And when the "Bread of Angels" becomes my food in Holy Communion, seal my heart forever against the suggestions of sinful plea-

sures. Finally, may I be among the number of those of whom Jesus spoke, "Blessed are the pure of heart for they shall see God." Amen.

Seek His purity in all you do, for blessed are the pure in heart.

Sitting with Our Lord at the Shore

1. We live in a culture "of the body" where gym memberships are on the rise. How do you see yourself? Do you focus on the outside or inside of who you are?
2. Our school sponsors a senior trip to Disney World every May. Weeks before departure, students diet and work out so they will be "ready" for the water events. Why? Do we foster a culture of vanity or inferiority from youth? Do we teach our young people to be comfortable with who they are?
3. The culture of "the body" teaches pleasure, while our faith teaches respect for God and others. Which one do you listen to?
4. Life is about relationships. We have both – a soul and a body. This makes us one. What happens when we look only at our soul apart from the body, the body apart from the soul? Do you recognize the problem with this?

7

United We Stand

In 2010, the choir I supervise was asked to sing at the Town of Hempstead September 11th Sunrise Memorial Service at Point Lookout, New York. The choir would sing as people arrived at the service, perform a meditation song as family members placed flowers at the memorial and sing as people left. During the song selection process, my assistant Christine and I stressed about how a choir that exclusively sang religious music could learn a whole new repertoire of patriotic songs. I called the Town Supervisor's office to have our song selection approved. I was surprised when I was told that they preferred that we sing our usual religious music and that our only consideration should be to remember the ecumenical spirit of the event. The separation of Church and State had been hammered into the American psyche for so long that I mistakenly assumed that the same philosophy would be upheld at this event.

As we sang on the beach on that cool September morning, it was obvious that many of the people in attendance were consoled in some manner through their connection with God.

The greatest error that we could have committed would have been omitting God from the service. With tears streaming down the worn and weary faces of the family members of those lost on that tragic day, the lifeline to God was clearly evident. A reminder that even in tragedy, God hears our pleas.

When members of the Sanhedrin began to conspire against Jesus, they sought ways to turn His followers and the Romans against Him. They cleverly devised questions that seem to have no correct answer. One such question was thrust upon the young teacher: "Is it lawful to pay taxes?" If Jesus urged His followers to pay taxes then He would be perceived as a Roman sympathizer. If He stated that everyone should avoid paying taxes, then the Romans would arrest Him as an insurrectionist. Jesus' brilliant reply, "Render to Caesar what is Caesar's and to God what is God's," should heighten our need for the presence of our Lord in society and especially government.

People defend the separation of Church and State as if these two entities should be mutually exclusive. We often forget that those seeking religious freedom founded our country. They never desired to push God out of the equation. The separation of Church and State deters religion from directly meddling in government matters. This does not mean that our government cannot acknowledge different aspects or expressions of the diverse faith denominations within our country. Many people in government or society in general have become God-phobic and especially Christophobic. This is causing us to whitewash religion from our society.

Thomas Jefferson spoke convincingly on the subject of including God in society:

And can the liberties of a nation be thought secure when we have removed their only firm basis, a conviction in the minds of the people that these liberties are the gift of God? That they are not to be violated but with His wrath? Indeed I tremble for my country when I reflect that God is just; that his justice cannot sleep forever.

> (*Notes on the State of Virginia* (Philadelphia: Matthew Carey, 1794), Query XVIII, p. 237)

Jefferson and the Founding Fathers would cringe at an America that pushed prayer out of its schools. The country they founded was not only a country that believed in God but included the teaching of Jesus Christ in its formation. Our sixth president, John Quincy Adams preached:

> [T]he birth-day of the nation is indissolubly linked with the birth-day of the Saviour [and] forms a leading even in the progress of the gospel dispensation..[T]he Declaration of Independence first organized the social compact on the foundation of the Redeemer's mission upon earth [and] laid the cornerstone of human government upon the first precepts of Christianity.
> (*An Oration delivered before the inhabitants of the town of Newburyport at their request on the Sixty-First Anniversary of the Declaration of Independence* [Newburyport: Charles Whipple, 1837], pp. 5-6)

The American Fathers recognized that their relationship with Jesus Christ had strengthened our foundation. They knew that without a clear guide, our country would go astray. President Obama updated the status of the American condition in a speech in 2007:

> Whatever we once were, we're no longer a Christian nation. At least not just. We are also a Jewish nation, a Muslim nation, and a Buddhist nation, a Hindu nation and a nation of nonbelievers.

Barack Obama was not incorrect in his assessment of our country. We have been willing to surrender our Christian principles and our Judeo-Christian identity. We consider the Ten Commandments as a religious edict rather than a moral code that should be written into the hearts of every person. Because the Decalogue originated in the Bible, it is dismissed by some people as religious propaganda. The nonbeliever has been allowed to share in holding the reins of the spiritual direction of our nation.

The American political system forces its citizens to choose which well-defined philosophical bin they want to reside. People reside at the polar ends of either Republican or Democrat, conservative or liberal. There is a perceived right or wrong based on how a party's platform is viewed. Membership in a particular party determines your stance on topics like abortion, universal health care, global warming, to name only a few of the topics that divide Americans. Individuals rationalize their personal beliefs based on what they have heard from the pundits and political evangelists. In the fury of political upheaval, we must not bypass the pursuit of truth when we choose our political alliances.

When we provide another person what is owed to them, it is considered justice. When Jesus simply exhorts us to give God and Caesar their respective due, He is recognizing one of the necessary characteristics of justice: truth. Spiritual blindness will cause an individual to ignore the truth in favor of subjective indulgence. This self-entitlement has bred the latest form of relativism. Relativism rejects the obvious truth and relies only on personal desire to formulate the set of rules that govern society and especially personal morality. The truth is only convenient if it fits into the plan of the individual. Without adherence to a strict moral code, we dangerously set sail into stormy waters without any type of navigational device.

As Americans, we constantly remind ourselves about the price of freedom. We pay homage to the men and women who gave the ultimate sacrifice for our country. But what is this gift of freedom all about? We often mistakenly define "freedom." When asked to explain their understanding of freedom, many people state that freedom is the ability to do whatever we please. Pope John Paul II clarified this when he stated, "Freedom is not doing what we want to do, but rather what we ought to do."

As Jesus held the Roman coin in His hand, He hoped to alert His disciples to the importance of fulfilling our earthly and heavenly obligations. It is not only a possibility, but also, a necessity to be a good citizen while being a faithful Christian. The ever-evolving notion of the separation of Church and State promotes the disposal of religious qualities from the resume of the model American. Like Barack Obama many people in our country have given equal status to the nonbeliever and allow them to set the American agenda.

The sacrificial nature of those who have given their lives in service of our country is not unlike the sacrificial nature of the cross. As our Founding Fathers constructed the guidelines of our great country in documents such as the Declaration of Independence and the Constitution, they consciously utilized Christ as their model. As Christian Americans, we should not cease to implement the life, teachings, Passion, Death and Resurrection of Jesus in our society not because of our religious affiliation but because of an adherence to the truth.

From experience, we know that discussions of religion and politics can create the perfect storm. We also understand that mixing religion and politics in the same discussion can be social suicide. We must not relent in our efforts in putting religion back into society even though those in the minority scream the loudest.

The exclusion of prayer from our public schools can be linked to the campaign commenced by atheist Madalyn Murray O'Hair. Incensed that her son William had been expected to learn the "Our Father" in school, O'Hair made it her mission to abolish prayer in public school. In his book, *My Life Without God,* William J. Murray spoke candidly of how he regretted his mother's decision to start the campaign against religion and encouraged him to live as an atheist. He had his conversion at thirty-three years of age.

Murray explained how he came to find Christ:

> But it was in this Bible that I found the truth about Jesus Christ, the truth that sets every man free. That truth is that Jesus had paid the price for my sin so I

could be reborn and be a new man and have the gift of eternal life. I learned that this gift was mine for the asking. All I had to do was repent of my sins and ask Christ into my life as Lord!

Today William Murray is a practicing Christian who crusades for religious freedom.

Each November we celebrate Thanksgiving to commemorate the voyage of the Pilgrims on the *Mayflower* and their gratitude for surviving the difficult winter of 1621. A pilgrim is a person who travels to a holy place so that they can worship God in the way that He deserves to be worshiped. The journey of the Pilgrims began in Europe but did not end at Plymouth Rock. The spiritual voyage of America continues today and must include Jesus Christ if we are to be successful as Americans and as Christians. We should protect our religious freedom at all cost.

Abraham Lincoln who rallied Americans for a national day of fasting and prayer wrote this proclamation to those who seemed to forget the place of God in America.

It is the duty of nations as well as of men to own their dependence upon the overruling power of God, and to confess their sins and transgressions in humble sorrow, yet with assured hope that genuine repentance will lead to mercy and pardon, and to recognize the sublime truth, announced in Holy Scripture, and proven by all history, that those nations only are blessed whose God is the Lord. And, insomuch (sic) as we know that by His divine law nations, like individuals, are subjected to punishments and chastisement in this world, may we not justly fear that the awful calamity of civil war which now desolates the land may be but a punishment inflicted upon us for our presumptuous sins, to the needful end of our national reformation as a whole people? We have been the recipients of the choicest bounties of Heaven; we have been preserved these many years in peace and prosperity; we have grown in numbers, wealth and power as no other nation has ever grown. But we have forgotten God. We have forgotten the gracious hand which has preserved us in peace and multiplied and enriched and strengthened us, and we have vainly imagined, in the deceitfulness of our hearts, that all these blessings were produced by some superior wisdom and virtue of our own. Intoxicated with unbroken success, we have become too self-sufficient to feel the necessity of redeeming and preserving grace, too proud to pray to the God that made us. It behooves us, then, to humble ourselves before the offended power, to confess our national sins and to pray for clemency and forgiveness. [March 30, 1863]

Our time at the shore should make us meditate on the privilege of living in such a beautiful country. We must also be mindful of our responsibility as American Christians to preserve the faith that has been handed on to us. The inclusion of religion is not an imposition, but an enhancement to society. We have witnessed firsthand what the exclusion of God has done to our government and schools. It is time to put Him in His rightful place. God permeates all things and must be included in all we do. Do not permit those who are insecure in their own belief to undermine your ability to practice and observe your faith as you wish. Too much has been sacrificed in the name of freedom. Let freedom ring and proclaim that God is alive in our country!

Sitting with Our Lord at the Shore

1. Reflecting on the shore of Point Lookout during the 9/11 Memorial always reminds me that we are a land of the free and home of the brave. It is God that makes us free. If the words "under God" were removed from the Pledge of Allegiance or "in God we trust" was removed from our coins, what would you do about it?
2. Our country is founded on the Judaic-Christian tradition. How do you deal with the God subject in your social circles? Do you integrate faith into your civic duties?
3. Certain Americans are doing everything in their power to eliminate faith from culture. Does the lack of prayer in our schools disturb you? What about removing Christ from Christmas or the government trying to limit our religious liberties?

8

Grounded in Love

In June of 1977, we met William for the first time in that summer in Rockaway Beach. William was the father of my cousin's friend. Even though there were many cousins on the beach, William managed to remember our names. He loved to walk by the shore. The exercise kept his mid-sixties body in solid shape. As the summer passed, William's forgetfulness began to manifest itself. He struggled to remember our names when we encountered him by the shore. Alzheimer's had begun to take control of William's mind.

By the next summer in 1978, the disease had pushed steadily through William's body. William's usual routine of walking by the ocean became an adventure, as he would lose his way. Concerned for his safety, my mother asked my cousin Terry and me to patrol the beach and return him to his family. After performing this task a few times, Terry and I would initiate the pursuit of William on our own. Even as teenagers, we comprehended the necessity of our actions. The relief on the face of William's wife served as reward enough for two boys who usually expected larger remuneration for a job well done.

In my second book, *Lessons from the Master*, I related the story of how my wife Allison suddenly dropped her chair and bag on the beach one day to assist a girl in need. Allison explained her motives as being prompted by her recent hearing of the parable of the Last Judgment at Mass. This powerful message in Matthew's Gospel can nudge even the most complacent soul to look for Jesus along the path of life.

Seeing Jesus Christ in the average person can be a daunting challenge. Our preoccupation with our own agenda can obscure the basic needs of our neighbor. Self-absorption may place blinders on us that we never know exist. The nature of the new age has stepped up the pace of our lives. We naturally worry about accomplishing the tasks that maintain order and prevent chaos from creeping into our world. This new obsession unfortunately deters us from integrating compassion into our lives when it is most necessary.

The word, "elevate," means to raise someone or something to a higher place. The ultimate goal of every relationship is to elevate the other people in our lives. Many of us are content to let our relationships remain in their current state. The edict of Christ to "love one another" includes raising the hearts and souls of others to be more like Jesus Himself. We are called by God to lift them in their despair, to clarify their scrutiny, to soften their hardened hearts and lead them to the truth. All of these are accomplished when we assume the role of Christ in daily living.

In his Letter to the Ephesians, Saint Paul presented some important insight to the Christian community:

May Christ dwell in your hearts through faith; that you, rooted and grounded in love, may have strength to comprehend with all the holy ones what is the breadth and length and height and depth and to know the love of Christ that surpasses knowledge, so that you may be filled with all the fullness of God. Now to him who is able to accomplish far more than all we ask or imagine, by the power at work within us, to him be glory in the Church and in Christ Jesus to all generations, forever and ever. Amen.

(Ephesians 3:17-21)

To be an actual disciple of Jesus requires us to practice the same love He practiced. This demands that we shed the prejudice, preconceived ideas, selfish will and other worldly intrusions that deter our active care and concern for others. Jesus did not allow the ebb and flow of emotions to change the path of His gracious mercy. If He did, we can assume that the betrayal, mockery, and other horrific events of Good Friday would have steered His heart in another direction. Instead, His love conquered all hatred.

Assuming the love of Christ is a full time proposition. Even while engaged by the leisure of the beach, we must be on guard to attend to the needs of others. How many times have you grabbed the hand of a stranger who became entangled in the vicious embrace of a wave that pushed him or her into a precarious situation? Perhaps you returned a child safely to his parents after he lost his way on the beach. Love takes no holiday. It must become our eternal obsession.

Spanish mystic Saint Teresa of Avila created a beautiful meditation of how we are now charged with becoming the human hands of Christ now that He has rejoined His Father in heaven. Christians are entrusted to act on His behalf:

Christ has no body now, but yours.
No hands, no feet on earth, but yours.
Yours are the eyes through which
Christ looks compassion into the world.
Yours are the feet
with which Christ walks to do good.
Yours are the hands
with which Christ blesses the world.

How we deal with this mission in this life will determine where we land in the next. Become obsessed with His love. Hold others with His hands. Show compassion with His heart. See others through His eyes. Run to those in need with His feet. On the beach, in the mall, on the parkway and on the street you can fulfill Christ's simplest wish – love.

Sitting with Our Lord at the Shore

1. Remember Cain's question, "Am I my brother's keeper?" In the parable of the Last Judgment Jesus reminds us that the answer is "yes." Reflect on how you have lived this out in your life.
2. We live in a world of calendars and control. Yet God laughs at our calendars and summons us to love by His interruptions in our daily life. How has God interrupted your day

and asked you to see how you have lived out the prayer of
St. Teresa of Avila in your life?
3. Relationship is critical to the life of faith. Do you elevate the
lives of others in your life? How?
4. Christianity is about seeing. How do you see others whom
you encounter during the course of the day?

9

The Inner Circle

When large groups gather at the beach, they often form a circle so that each person can interact with the others. The collection of umbrellas is carefully arranged so they provide shade while not being an intrusion into the conversations. Some of my fondest memories revolve around our family's gatherings in Rockaway Beach, New York as a child. Those in attendance regularly on Beach 111th Street left enough space for us to accommodate more than thirty people in our weekly reunions. The nineteen cousins would eventually divide into their cliques by age while the adults filled each other in on the news of the week. My grandparents sat upon their throne-like, high-back chairs and relished every minute of the activities.

Family is an integral part of the beach experience. Sandcastle building, swimming, endless sporting options and being the perfect venue for communication lures millions of families to the beach each year. But time changes every family. Sometimes they change for the better and sometimes for the worse. Children grow up and start their own families. Some move away to take advantage of job opportunities. But there may be some other things that are completely out of our control that alter family relationships.

The death of my grandfather, my aunt and cousin dramatically altered the beach scene for my family during the 1960's and 1970's. When my grandmother passed away in 1980, Rockaway would never be the same. Many of my cousins still reside in Rockaway Beach, but our time together has faded into glorious memories.

Every time my feet touch the sand, the shadows of Rockaway Beach still follow me. I vividly recall the waves and the adults teaching us how to swim; the various card games and learning how to think strategically; having real conversation with grown-ups that exceeded my usual one-word answers in which I would respond. But most of all I remember the laughter and understanding the importance of being together.

Even though no relationship is easy, familial interaction can be the most challenging. Because we are born into a family, we are cemented into these bonds. So we attempt to make them work as best as we can. The more difficult relationships require more compromise. They demand we give more than we take. We may have to speak less and listen more. People often walk away from relationships that drain them of time and energy. Sometimes the distance between people and the passage of years can cause drifting apart. It is never too late to kick start a stagnant relationship.

After teaching for more than thirty years, I am convinced that every person assumes the role of teacher at various points in his or her life. Many important lessons were presented to me at the beach. It is the perfect place to demonstrate how we absorb valuable gifts to help us live properly even when we least expect it. As we proceed through this chapter, we would like to reflect on how we affect our families in a positive way. What lessons can we learn from our time together?

One of the major lessons of family can be learned from the early Christians:

> The community of believers was of one heart and mind, no one claimed that any of his possessions was his own, but they had everything in common.
>
> (Acts 4:32)

The "me first" philosophy divides many families and individuals. Narcissism causes us to live for individual goals rather than to think and live for the good of the whole group.

Successful families understand that much more can be accomplished while working as a united group.

The self-centered attitude often leads to the dismissal of an active faith life. I pose this question to my students on retreats: "Who is the spiritual leader of your family?" Because the majority of Christians struggle with faithfulness to Mass, I expand this question to ask who is the person behind whether the family attends Mass on Sunday, or is the person that leads the family in bypassing the act of worship.

Faith, very much like love, is built by practice. When you least desire to engage in these two important acts, it is when they required the most effort. Families need a leader in faith. Someone is needed to initiate grace at meals or to decide when you will attend Mass together. Active participation demands diligence and perseverance. Getting dressed for church is low on the list of priorities on a hot, sticky summer day when the beach, lake or pool beckons. Someone in your family needs to live by example.

Are you the spiritual force in your family or do you allow Sunday to float by without putting God on the schedule? It is not always a popular choice when free time is lean and the agenda is full. Individuals rationalize Mass attendance as a man-made entity. However, the edicts to gather each Sunday clearly come directly from our Savior:

> For where two or three are gathered together in my name, there am I in the midst of them.
> (Matthew 18:20)

> Then he took the bread, said the blessing, broke it, and gave it to them, saying, "This is my body, which will be given for you; do this in memory of me." And likewise the cup after they had eaten, saying, "This cup is the new covenant in my blood, which will be shed for you."
> (Luke 22:19-20)

As in any relationship, Jesus desires our companionship and offers us communion with Him. Fusion with our Lord is certainly possible if we desire it.

My own kids would dread my announcement for the time on Sunday that we would attend church. This earned me the nickname "the church police." Recently they started making their own preferences known for which Mass they wanted to attend. It is no longer a fight about if, but when we will go to Mass.

Practice makes perfect as the old adage explains. The family that prays together usually has a keener sense of what relationships mean. With God at the center, all other relationships assume a higher place in the order of life.

No family can survive without forgiveness. The more time we spend together, the more apt we are to hurt or offend the ones we supposedly love the most. The act of forgiveness expects us to overlook a bruised ego even before it has time to heal. We may not know the immediate benefits of reconciling a relationship because the pain or sting of heartbreak may be too vivid in our minds to actually feel as if we have fixed the problem. But the initial act of forgiveness may be what was needed to prevent the wrongdoing from pushing the relationship over the cliff into oblivion.

Jesus perfected His lesson on forgiveness. In His guideline for prayer in the Our Father, He demonstrated that we must forgive in order to be forgiven:

> Forgive us our trespasses as we forgive those who trespass against us.

Jesus reinforces this petition on Good Friday when He excuses the unthinkable treachery of His conspirators and executioners as He compassionately urges His Father to "forgive them for they know not what they do."

Forgiveness should promote change within a relationship. It should emerge as an influential teacher and aid us in becoming more loving people. To say "I'm sorry" is an empty statement if we do not alter our own behavior.

If you are married and have your own family, the demands of your personal time have multiplied. You tend to the concerns of your spouse and children while maintaining the relationship of your birth family. A quick glance at our family reveals why we have become the people we are today. We may have inherited the obstinacy of our father, the sense of humor of our mother or the talent of a grandparent. We never escape the family that runs within our veins. Our personalities have evolved through our genes as well as what we have witnessed in our developmental years.

Every family has a uniting influence. This person works behind the scenes to organize the events that pull the family back together. Unfortunately, too much time elapses between natural gatherings like weddings and funerals. Many families drift apart as schedules collide. We swear that we will make a more concerted effort to gather, but we seldom fulfill this promise.

Keeping a family together requires full time maintenance. There are days when we wish we can bi-locate so that we can fulfill all the demands of the people in our life. We juggle our relationships and are exhausted by the perpetual balancing act that we are forced to execute.

Our family provides unmatched comfort to us. Underneath its worn exterior lies a place that we know and love despite its imperfections. Just as the early Christians found strength in one another, we must rely on the center of all community, the family. Make your family a priority.

Sitting with Our Lord at the Shore

1. The family is a small church where children are first nurtured on faith. Does your family pray and attend Mass together? What lessons have you taught your family?
2. Sometimes the beach gets rough and the waves can knock you down. Relationships and family life also have their rough moments where things go wrong. How have you practiced forgiveness in your family? Are there any relationships that need reconciling?
3. We are called to shepherd each other in the ways of faith. Who sets the spiritual tone in your family? Does your family have any goals in the area of faith?
4. The beach experience can bring your family together. Has this been your experience? If not, what type of places serve as quality time experiences?

10

An Awesome God

The main attraction at the shore is obviously the ocean. The ocean lures beach-goers not only for swimming, but for its beauty as well. Admirers gaze at the ocean for hours. The light dances upon the water causing the landscape to constantly change. Vibrant greens and blues emerge from the murky grays in reaction to its partner the sky.

One of the most intriguing qualities of the ocean is its expansiveness. The infinite edge of the ocean disappears beyond the horizon. We attempt to grasp the magnitude and breadth of its size, but as we walk in the foam of the exhausted waves, we are like one grain of sand on the beach in comparison to the massive body of water.

We usually do not place lakes on the same scale as the ocean but if you have ever flown over the Great Lakes you understand the immense size of these bodies of water. You believe as if you are crossing the ocean as you peek out of the airplane window and see only water for miles. Some larger lakes share the ferocious nature of the ocean. The calm, gentle waves have the ability to transform into an angry beast. The rocky waters of these larger bodies of water have swallowed even the largest of boats.

As a fisherman on the Sea of Galilee, Simon Peter had survived many storms. They were part of his business. Strong winds would blow down from the mountains around the lake causing storms to erupt. Peter and Andrew learned to adapt to the weather. On the day that Jesus asked His disciples to set sail, they must have assumed that it would be a routine crossing of the lake. The storm that occurred this day must have been stronger than any other one that Peter had encountered.

There are two contrasting scenes upon the boat. One scene depicts the apostles fighting for their lives. The boat had taken on water and was in danger of sinking. The men scrambled to bail water from the vessel to prevent capsizing. Then, on the other hand, there is Jesus serenely sleeping in His corner in the boat.

The apostles woke Jesus, "Master, Master, we are perishing!" Christ arose and dealt with the most troubling problem first. He rebuked the wind and the waves. Immediately, calm was restored. Then our Lord directed His anger and concern towards His friends. "Where is your faith?" He scolded them. The apostles focused more on the amazing power displayed by the Teacher than His rhetorical slap down. Their only response was, "Who then is this, who commands even the winds and the sea and they obey him?"

The apostles play an important role in the Gospels. They are vital instruments in salvation history for many reasons:

1. They are witnesses to the risen Christ.
2. They are the first recipients of the Good News.

3. They link the twelve tribes of Israel with Jesus Christ's new Church.
4. Even though they were given a front row seat into the Passion, Death and Resurrection, they still struggled with their faith like every other Christian who was not given the same privilege.

Saint Thomas always comes to mind when we think of people who ignored the message of Christ. But the "doubting apostle" has plenty of company. Like the apostles, we forget who is in the boat with us. When problems arise, we lose our trust in God. We desire more concrete reassurance. We neglect the fact that His mere presence changes everything. Without an awareness of Christ, minor obstacles seem impassible.

Faith for some people is a tall order. Just as some fear swimming into the ocean because he or she cannot see what lurks beneath the surface, others refuse to believe because they do not view the entire picture clearly. The epistle addressed to the Hebrews explains faith:

Faith is the realization of what is hoped for and evidence of things not seen. (Hebrews 11:1)

Humans are stimulated by the senses. We search for the video or sound bite to confirm a news story or celebrity rumor. It dispels our doubts and puts the pieces of the story together. Faith requires bypassing the senses and allowing the heart to speak to us.

The human capacity has trouble comprehending the infinite nature of God. Faith allows many to believe in the existence of God, but our limited nature distorts His infinite abilities. Contemplating and gazing upon our Creator's magnificent oceans and lakes should provide a glimpse into the all-knowing and all-powerful and ever present God. The great depths of these waters and billions of creatures that dwell within them are minute in comparison to the awesomeness of God.

There is so much that remains unseen and unknown underneath the surface of the water. But yet, we never hesitate to believe that certain life exists in the ocean even though we do not see it. Why, then, do we constantly second-guess the possibility of God?

With such a magnificent creation before us, we should use our time at the shore to meditate on our own purpose. Why has God put me here? What is my vocation in this life? How am I supposed to influence the people around me? Like the ocean, because it is always there before us, we take certain things for granted. We fail to recognize the beauty of this life and its worth.

Looking out into the distant horizon always causes me to meditate on the daring adventures of my immigrant grandparents who left family behind to search for a better life in America. One element became a common denominator for all my grandparents who made this long voyage from Italy and Ireland. This element was faith. The transatlantic journey was daunting but was overshadowed by heartache and loneliness once they arrived at Ellis Island and settled into their new home in America. I often imagine them on the deck of a ship and fixating on the endless horizon and fearing the unknown that loomed ahead. But their relationship with God was mightier than any ocean. Their desolation was eased by the comfort of their Heavenly Father.

The powerful ocean demands respect. Even those who wade in the shallowest of waters must be aware of the dangerous currents below. Those who ignore basic rules of the sea can literally find themselves in troubled waters. Sadly, the headlines often relate stories of swimmers and boaters who perish because they did not heed the warning signs.

The all-powerful God also needs respect. The relationship with our Heavenly Father is built on demonstrating reverence. Unfortunately many of us approach this relationship with our own set of rules of worship. We often dismiss that we must enter into this relationship with our Lord with the reverence He deserves. Because of the human will, we hate restrictions. But our lives must have boundaries. The subjective world desires to play by its own rules. Without obedience to the simple guidelines set forth by our Creator, we will surely be adrift. God chooses the course; it is up to us to follow His guidance.

The magnificence of the ocean reminds us that God awaits our devotion and admiration. His awe draws us to Him. Use His creation to fill your life with wonder. Gaze upon the ocean, lake and infinite grains of sand to contemplate His place as the Alpha and Omega, the beginning and end of all things. Permit the mystery of nature to confirm the reality of His existence. Plunge the unknown depths. And discover what lies beneath.

Sitting with Our Lord at the Shore

1. In a canticle from the prophet Daniel, we recall that all creation praises the Lord. How does the magnificence of nature show you the existence of God? Has the beach helped you connect to God?

2. Every person has received a vocation from God. With each vocation there is an individual mission. Sometimes we know what it is, other times we may have to wait and learn it in the next life. What do you think your purpose is in this life?

3. The life of faith is about relationship. Who are the people who have sacrificed the most to get you where you are today? Who has influenced you the most in a positive way?

11

Survival of the Fittest

Sea gulls are often regarded as the most annoying pests at the beach. These familiar birds often invade food supplies of vacant beach camps. Recently, I witnessed a brazen gull swoop down and snatch a sandwich from a young girl as she ate her lunch.

In Breezy Point, the natural nemesis to beachgoers is the tern. These aggressive birds instinctively protect their eggs when a perceived predator approaches their nest. During the off-season, the terns lay their eggs close to the unused summer pathways. As the beach season begins, the protective birds that have become accustomed to the peace and quiet of the winter attack unsuspecting residents. The walk to the beach is especially treacherous in the days of late May and early June. The birds swoop down and attempt to peck at anyone who approaches their habitat.

On occasion, the tern switches his attention to the seemingly innocent seagulls. The mellower gulls usually ignore their more belligerent beach mates. However, one day I witnessed a tern interfering with the fishing ritual of a larger seagull. The gull, not in the mood to deal with a smaller bird, quickly disposed of the tern with his extremely strong beak.

The birds that dwell at the beach follow the same code of "survival of the fittest" that governs the rest of the animal kingdom. Humans have followed suit as we have constructed our world around the art of competition. The corporate, academic, sports and entertainment realms have all adopted the philosophy that only the strongest survive. Many of us are desensitized to the cutthroat approach taken to advance in society. We are willing to push others aside in order to achieve our goals. We are very aware of the power brokers and weaker players in the game as we plot our next move. We respect some because of his or her authority while we manipulate others because of their weakness. Our relationships become utilitarian and we judge another by his or her usefulness to us.

Jesus did not buy into the survival of the fittest mentality. As the King of Kings, and Master of All Creation He could have exerted His power and authority at any time. But instead, He took the simplest form as a poor, humble carpenter from Nazareth. His actions spoke much louder than His words and yet we know how powerful His words were. Jesus was keenly aware of the rich and influential, the powerful and mighty in His society. Yet, He gravitated to the lost and unwanted. The only fame that the companions of Jesus possessed was their notoriety for sin. These were the people who were not only cast aside, but also trampled upon at every opportunity. In the world where only the strongest succeeded, Jesus knew that these people needed His generosity and benevolence the most.

The apostles were extremely conscious of status in their

world. As the popularity of Jesus increased, so did their noto-riety. But with a constant discussion of the Kingdom of Heaven, they wondered what role status held in the next life. They asked Jesus, "Who is the greatest in the Kingdom of Heaven?" Jesus brought a child before His friends and stated, "Whoever humbles himself like this child is the greatest in the Kingdom of Heaven. And whoever receives one child such as this in my name, receives me." Surely, instead of presenting a simple child, the disciples expected the teacher to rattle off a list of prophets and kings. But rather than mention the most famous in biblical history, He pointed to the weakest member in society.

The Gospels provide a three-year snapshot into the adult life of Christ. As our Lord was providing the foundation of His Church, He presented the perfect pattern of human behavior. Instead of shoving the weakest aside, He welcomed them into His inner circle. This behavior infuriated the Pharisees and Sadducees who wanted to eliminate the influence of Jesus. They wanted Jesus to play by their rules. When He resisted, they plotted to remove Him from the game. The Teacher refused to socialize with the power-brokers. He saw through their hypocrisy and pursued sincere relationships with real people.

If we follow the example of Jesus, we invite rather than eliminate, we actively incorporate others into our lives instead of wondering how to manipulate them. The powerless must be strengthened by the stronger. Instead of pushing aside the feeble, we should usher them with us through the struggles of life. Those with talent must help them in cultivating the skills necessary to survive. Sharing our gifts with others can provide tremendous self-satisfaction.

As co-creators with the Father, others can mirror our talents as we assist them in cultivating theirs. Jesus urged His disciples to care for the "least of their brothers." The Teacher understood our inclination to achieve our goals at any cost. Our desires are skewed when we mistakenly love objects and use people. Our focus on the ultimate prize obscures the dignity of those we bypass in its pursuit.

The champions of the poor and forgotten are fortified by their efforts. The process of assisting others provides a source of strength that we cannot realize on our own. Generosity, compassion and empathy are all important components in our self-evolution as human beings. This transformation will not take place when we use our subjective will against others.

The Christian spin on "survival of the fittest" requires the strongest to carry the weakest, the mighty to uphold the lowly, the steady to counsel the troubled. Jesus, God made man, became the Good Shepherd to gather the misguided. His entrance into humanity brings the lost back into the fold. If His actions are the perfect pattern for us to emulate, we must reconsider our pursuit of our goals in the light of Christian love.

Sitting with Our Lord at the Shore

1. We all have a competitive side. Does your competitive side bring out the best or worst in you?
2. A biblical message reminds us to love people and use things. Our culture has a different message where it tells us to love things and use people. Do you approach your relationships as utilitarian?

3. Jesus makes it clear that the person with more talents is called to be more responsible. How do you treat those who are weaker and more helpless than you?

4. Jesus was interested in honest, genuine relationships. He had trouble dealing with those who identified themselves by what they had – power, privilege and status, rather than who they were. What do you look for in a relationship? Are you taken up with the externals or can you love others with strength and limitations?

12

Treasures in Our Midst

As I melt into my beach chair during the summer months, not everyone around me relishes the same opportunity to do absolutely nothing. The beach offers a relaxing atmosphere that may be too passive for some people. My wife Allison gets jumpy after an extended period of inactivity at the shore. She encourages our family to walk to the "point" of the Rockaway peninsula. Along the way, Allison and the kids attempt to find a potpourri of shells and sea glass.

The living creatures of the sea produce some magnificent shells. Mollusks, conch, scallops, oysters, mussels and clams yield an abundance of treasures by the ocean's edge. Sea glass comes from broken bottles cast upon the shore. After months and years of churning in the sandy brine, smooth and colorful masterpieces appear.

These shoreline treasures will not make anyone rich; however, they bring immediate smiles to the explorer who discovers them amidst the crashing waves. My wife and kids have returned from many an excursion rejoicing about their newly acquired prizes. They immediately take their shells and sea glass and pack them so they can be proudly displayed in our house at a later time. These seaside discoveries are the perfect illustration of how beauty is in the eye of the beholder. Many people walk past the same shells and pay little mind to their presence while others actively seek them.

There are also people in our midst daily whom we take for granted when they should be the center of our attention. Our relationships are the only personal possessions that we take from this life into the next. When we arrive at the gates of heaven our pockets are emptied of material goods. According to the Master, we will be judged by how we interacted with those we confront during our earthly existence. Jesus spoke about the hungry, the thirsty, the lonely, the imprisoned, and the sick. But what happens when we ignore those who know us best? These people may hunger and thirst in different ways than our eyes have become accustomed to searching. How have the people who should be the most essential elements of our lives become invisible or even disposable?

In an earlier chapter, we dealt with familial relationships and the difficulties that arise. Relationships can become strained on any level. Friends may drift apart because of unsaid resentments. Brothers and sisters can separate because of unconscious jealousy. Relationships are far more fragile than the most delicate of shells. Depending on past history, some must be treated with more care than others. Our objective in this chapter is to awaken our need for interaction and to utilize the individuals that God has placed among us. We should dedicate time making them a top priority in our lives just as we search for gems along the seashore.

Relationships require our consciousness. Consciousness jolts the human mind and body from autopilot and demands our heightened awareness. No longer should we be oblivious to the faces that require our attention. Just as we are instructed to pan our eyes left to right as we drive, we should do the same as we move throughout our day. No relationship can be successful when we are only focused on ourselves. The ego drives the individual to be consumed about the self; however, relationships require us to focus outward. The people that fail to move outside of themselves gain very little from their relationships.

One of the key elements of a relationship is recognizing the needs of the other people involved with us. The nonstop pace of our society and our dependency on technology diverts our attention from authentic encounters. We talk, but seldom communicate. Because of this constant motion we neglect the problem of loneliness.

Some individuals do not even realize their own isolation and seclusion from the rest of the community. Mother Teresa explained, "Loneliness and the feeling of being unwanted is the most terrible poverty." We can sit in a crowded room and still be lonely. We often assume that being present is sufficient. Without a connection to those who surround us, physical presence means nothing. Great theologian and writer Gilbert Keith Chesterton defined the importance of even one relationship:

> There are no words to express the abyss between isolation and having one ally. It may be conceded to the

mathematician that four is twice two. But two is not twice one; two is two thousand times one.

The great Christian author urges us to cherish the most profound of human gifts.

Our culture concentrates on the bottom line and cost of every action. It attempts to facilitate the most menial tasks so we do not waste any unnecessary motion. Efficiency is perceived as the key to happiness and fulfillment. Contrary to this, our relationships demand an extraordinary amount of time and effort.

All of our strength and energy should be exerted tending to our relationships. It is through these relationships that we will meet the face of the compassionate Christ. Faith will be found in our relationships when doubt sweeps over us. These people will assist us in experiencing infinite joy. Their caring hearts shall ease our mourning.

There is truly strength in numbers. Many seek and discover companionship, friendship and consolation in their churches, communities and organizations. These associations complement their friendships and familial relationships. People join these groups for more than "belonging to something." They discover their meaning in their connection to others.

The value of friendship, companionship and family is priceless. As we wait for the waves to reveal the next pristine treasure, we may want to glance at the gems that walk beside us on the shore to expose our potentially most exquisite possessions. Take the time to assess the significance of your family and friends. Look for the treasure that God has bestowed upon you to discover fulfillment and ultimate happiness.

Sitting with Our Lord at the Shore

1. Where do we go to help others? Usually nowhere! The person in front of you is God's will for you. Just open your eyes. Are you aware of all of the people around you, not just the important ones? Are there relationships in your life that need attention?

2. There's an Italian saying that explains "it is sweet to do nothing." A place where we can just "be." Why is this healthy?

3. Simple moments like collecting seashells with others can bring a certain joy. We treasure the experience more than the shells. What experiences do you treasure?

4. "No man is an island." But that is not always our experience. Have you experienced isolation and loneliness? Has this made you more aware of the needs of others?

13

When All Fails, Hope!

As I started to put the finishing touches on this book in the fall of 2012, Hurricane Sandy hit the east coast of the United States. As the meteorologists began to formulate their forecasts, terms like "Frankenstorm" and "the perfect storm" enhanced their ominous predictions. Like every other storm projection, the veteran old salt took it in stride. My mother often speaks of riding out many hurricanes in Rockaway Beach and staying put even when the Atlantic Ocean and Jamaica Bay met. Stormy forecasts seldom ran these people out of town because they had literally seen it all. I charged my laptop so that the certain blackout would not deter me from my nightly writing. But as the hurricane and its effects overpowered the New York metropolitan area, I changed my plans for this section of the book.

Hurricane Sandy unfortunately lived up to the hype and wreaked enormous havoc upon most of the tri-state area of New York, New Jersey and Connecticut. Winds during the storm howled and trees in our neighborhood toppled liked dominos. The news reported the devastation, especially from the shore areas. I expected to hear the usual stories of people who had to pump water from their basements. Then neighbors began to inquire about our bungalow in Breezy Point. They spoke about a fire that had spread during the height of the storm. Initially reports stated that fifty homes were lost, but after an official accounting was taken, more than one hundred homes had burnt to the ground.

The fire had started only a few blocks from our bungalow and in a community where only a few feet exist between houses I was not sure that our modest summer home had survived. The aerial pictures of the destruction indicated that ten blocks of homes were affected. So, accompanied by my son, Alex, I ventured to the beach to make my own observations. When I arrived in Breezy Point, I passed through the flurry of police and security checkpoints and encountered some friendly, but distraught faces. They had already surveyed their personal damage and had familiarized themselves with the surrounding tragedy. They informed me that my usual route was impassable and that I must take the promenade if I wanted an unobstructed trail to our bungalow.

As Alex and I ventured through the remaining water and piles of sand, we encountered the face of the devastation. Two story homes were flipped on their sides, wooden decks had been removed from moorings and bungalows shifted from their foundations like an angry giant had been let loose through the community. We, like the others who walked past us, could not speak. After my brief tour, I realized that the houses that were destroyed in the fire were only part of the desolation. The picture on the previous page shows the remains of the favorite hangout of Breezy Point residents, "The Sugar Bowl," a small bar only a few hundred feet from the shore. Only one outdoor table and a chain link fence remained in the rubble.

One picture in the news concentrated on the only remaining possession of a homeowner, a statue of the Blessed Mother. This striking image reminded me of the amazing faith of the people in this beach-front community. I thought of others shaken in their belief like those closest to Jesus after His crucifixion. The apostles had quickly forgotten about their friend's predictions of resurrection and new life. Instead of anticipating His impending glory, they retreated and hid in the upper room.

Within a few days after the death of Jesus the vision of humanity changes. No longer are we bound by the usual confines of life and death. The Resurrection of Christ smashes those parameters forever. Hope reigns supreme. Even when situations seem impossible, the power of Christ tells a different story. Our expectations suddenly soar when the actions of the risen Jesus exclaimed, "We have nothing to lose!"

Christianity offers a unique optic. No matter how difficult life becomes, the infinite mercy of God provides hope. The modern individual is preoccupied by immediate gratification rather than long-term gain. We often become so entrenched in the moment that we forget about the eternal possibilities promised to us by the Savior.

But hope is not a possibility without a relationship with God. It is the first step in charting a course with the virtue of hope. This means that we not only seek knowledge of Jesus Christ, but also, actively fuse Him to our every action. Pope Benedict XVI addressed this question in his encyclical *Spe Salvi* (*Saved In Hope*):

We have raised the question: can our encounter with the God who in Christ has shown us his face and opened his heart be for us too not just "informative" but "performative" – that is to say, can it change our lives, so that we know we are redeemed through the hope that it expresses? (*Spe Salvi*, #4)

The Pope urges us to differentiate between simply learning about Jesus and allowing His actions to permeate our daily lives. Thus, will we "walk the walk" or be content to "talk the talk"? Ultimately, we have some serious choices to make.

But this requires faith, faith in the face of adversity, tragedy and pain. One way to separate those individuals who can transcend suffering from those who buckle under the pressure brought about by misfortune, is to determine those with faith:

"And what does faith give you?"
"Eternal life."
According to this dialogue, the parents were seeking access to the faith for their child, communion with believers, because they saw in faith the key to "eternal life." Today as in the past, this is what being baptized, becoming Christians, is all about: it is not just an act of socialization within the community, not simply a welcome into the Church. The parents expect more for the one to be baptized: they expect that faith, which includes the corporeal nature of the Church and her sacraments, will give life to their child – eternal life. Faith is the substance of hope.
(*Spe Salvi*, #10)

When All Fails, Hope!

Faith says, "I may not understand why this has happened, but with the help from God I can emerge from the rubble." For those who have experienced catastrophe, they understand how difficult it may be to utter these words. But if he or she has placed their hope in the Lord, they have felt the grace enveloped in hope.

In desperate times, many people call upon the apostle Saint Jude Thaddeus to intercede for them. He is known as the patron saint of hopeless cases. This novena is prayed once each day for nine days:

> Most holy Apostle, Saint Jude, faithful servant and friend of Jesus, the Church honors and invokes you universally, as the patron of difficult cases, of things almost despaired of, pray for me, I am so helpless and alone. Intercede with God for me that He brings visible and speedy help where help is almost despaired of. Come to my assistance in this great need that I may receive the consolation and help of heaven in all my necessities, tribulations, and sufferings, particularly –
>
> (Make your request here)
>
> – and that I may praise God with you and all the saints forever. I promise, O Blessed Saint Jude, to be ever mindful of this great favor granted me by God and to always honor you as my special and powerful patron, and to gratefully encourage devotion to you. Amen.

When you find yourself pushed into a corner, raise your eyes to heaven for help. Grab hold of the hope of the Risen Christ when the situation seems to have no outlet. Make this the moment to put your faith on the line. Have hope!

Sitting with Our Lord at the Shore

1. Hurricanes happen! Reflect on the hurricanes that have disturbed your life and smashed into your comfort zone. How did you react?

2. No one can change reality. However, we can change our attitudes to the reality of our lives. Does your faith help you to see this world and its challenges in a different way?

3. Overwhelmed? Lost in the dark? Consumed by anger? These can be normal reactions to painful and difficult circumstances. How have you dealt with things when you felt that hope was a million miles away?

4. "I may not understand why this has happened but with help from God I can emerge from the rubble." How has your relationship with Jesus ushered you into the virtue of hope?

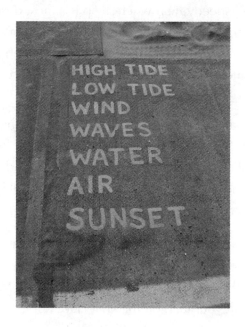

14

God Gives, God Takes

Looking for the right location to sit at the beach is one of the most important elements of the beach experience. Some people avoid the crowds by moving their umbrella and chair closer to the water. Problems with this decision occur when the tide begins to rise and these people are soon fighting the rushing tide. Initially, what seemed like a smart move now has entire families scrambling for drier ground. We have all been surprised by a wave that has snuck up on us and soaked our towels and other beach gear.

If you go to the beach frequently in the summer, you may be aware of the tide schedules. I often hear people ask others about the time of high tide. The above picture is a chart on the sidewalk that a diligent resident of Breezy Point fills in each day. The rising and falling of the tide is an example of how the momentum of life constantly changes.

Beachgoers are often warned against the dangers of rip currents. A riptide literally sucks a person into deeper water. Because the swimmer is helpless against the force of the ocean, he is advised to allow the current to pull him out into stiller waters if he cannot initially escape its embrace. The first instinct of a swimmer may be to panic. Fear may cause the swimmer to exert too much energy and fighting the riptide will only cause exhaustion. The swimmer must seek a way out of the current and swim away from the riptide by moving parallel to the shore. Once the swimmer has regained his composure and strength, he can start to swim diagonally back to shore.

The riptide is an excellent analogy for life. The person who assumes that he or she has all of their plans in order is usually mistaken. Even when we know that high tide is about to arrive, we may not be ready for it. Unlike the tides that are predictable, the highs and lows of life are not. Tragedy often seems to catch individuals unaware. We ride high on the wave of life one moment and are thrown into the depths the next. Like being overcome by the rip current, our first reaction may be to panic. No one likes losing control. We are terrible "backseat drivers." We desire to have our hands on the wheel at all times and steer our own course. While rotating within the uncomfortable currents of life that sweep us to places unknown, we must place our trust in God. Psalm 18 has become a mantra for many seeking solace in the Lord:

> I love thee, O LORD, my strength.
> The LORD is my rock, and my fortress, and my deliverer,
> my God, my rock, in whom I take refuge,
> my shield, and the horn of my salvation, my stronghold.
> I call upon the LORD, who is worthy to be praised,
> and I am saved from my enemies.
> The cords of death encompassed me,

the torrents of perdition assailed me;
the cords of Sheol entangled me,
the snares of death confronted me.
In my distress I called upon the LORD;
to my God I cried for help.
From his temple he heard my voice,
and my cry to him reached his ears.   (Psalm 18:1-6)

The author of this famous passage was David whom God had saved from the "clutches" of King Saul. Like David when we face the dangers of being assailed, entangled and confronted, we must put our trust in God as well. Every beachgoer at one time has participated in building sand castles. Deeply involved in our project we are oblivious to the waves about to challenge our latest masterpiece or fortress. The mightiest structure, however, is no match for the momentum of the ocean. No matter what we do, we will not be able to change our situation. We will never be able to predict our future, but we always command our reactions and attitudes. Prayer and our connection with God will weigh heavily on these as well.

The Book of Job in the Old Testament beautifully illustrates the courageous response to the dramatic changes in life. In this story, after the devil noticed that God's servant Job has remained faithful, the devil believed that it is because of his good fortune. Satan urges God to strip Job of his children, livestock and fortune to see if he will reverse his attitude towards God under duress. Even after Job is rendered unrecognizable when he is covered with boils and sores, the loyal servant praised God rather than cursing him. The ever patient Job exclaims:

Naked I came forth from my mother's womb, and na-
ked shall I go back again. The LORD gave and the
LORD has taken away; blessed be the name of the
LORD!   (Job 1:21)

The story of Job may be an extreme didactic tale of suffering, but it should make us mindful of God's presence in our
joyful existence. As we experience the peaks and valleys of life,
we often blame God for the causes and effects of these changes.
Evil and suffering are always intertwined within the discussion of
God. Like the tides, these elements of life are part of the natural
occurrences of the world that the Creator has set into motion.
We must look to Job for guidance. Without God, true joy is not
possible. With God beside us, we have given ourselves an edge
to overcome any difficulty that is set before us.

The tides should teach us the importance of moderation.
We can be close enough to the ocean or the lake to obtain a gor-
geous view, but far enough away to avoid getting soaked when
the tides change. The "all or nothing" mentality causes many
people to dive into situations until they are in way too deep. Because our culture encourages us to soak in as much as we can,
we gorge ourselves in all aspects of life. We eat, drink, spend
and play without thinking about the consequences or whether or
not we are actually enjoying our current activity. Peace and calm
are usually found when we find middle ground.

Those successful in their relationships understand that
compromise is an art. Every person seeks validation of his ideas
and feelings. Relationships regularly require us to reevaluate our
position on a certain subject or situation because of the views
of those around us. Just as we desire to be recognized and ap-

preciated, compromise reduces the presence of our notions and beliefs so that the will of others may emerge.

The changing tides remind us that the world is in constant motion. It evolves with or without our permission or acknowledgment. As humans grow, they also change and our faith lives must evolve as well. Ponder the rising and falling of your spiritual development as you watch the changing of the tides. Do you allow your Christian faith to surround others or do you permit it to vanish as quickly as the departing tide? Use your faith life to provide stability in the turbulent moments especially when troubles rush you like the mounting waves. Prayer and faith may be the only weapons against the chaos around you. Let the love of Christ embrace you like the breaking waves that blanket the sandy shore.

Sitting with Our Lord at the Shore

1. The tide rises and the tide falls just like life experiences. Elements in life, like riptides, pull us to places where we do not want to go. How do you deal with the surprise of the unknown?
2. We like control. The word is not in God's vocabulary. Keeping control is like fighting a riptide. Do you ever just "let go" and let God act in your life?
3. Fear or stress can be worry without God. All depends on you, unless you extend an invitation to God to help you in your needs. Are you at your best or worst when stressed?
4. Trace the highs and lows of your spiritual life. How has your faith life changed over the past few years?
5. One author says, "To live is to suffer and to survive is to find meaning in suffering." Reflect on this in terms of your own suffering in life.

15

The Setting Sun

During my childhood, my parents wanted to extract the most out of our beach day. This often meant that we would not leave the beach until the sun had set. The early evening is one of the most peaceful times of the day at the shore. The exhausting heat of the day now gives way to cooler breezes. The chairs rotate toward the setting sun as we admire the spectacular show.

Because God understands our attraction to the worldly, He tantalizes our senses with natural beauty. His most fascinating teachers used the natural and even man-made items around us to connect us to the Divine. The Church uses sacramentals in worship. A sacramental is usually an object that has been blessed and is associated with liturgical celebrations and rites. Jesus and many saints built a bridge between the worldly and the divine by developing their theology around what I refer to as "secular sacramentals." Jesus utilized sheep, seeds and coins in His parables. The tradition of Saint Patrick describes that he evangelized using the sun and the shamrock. Saint Boniface supposedly employed the tree to connect pagan people to Christ.

These material objects draw us into worship of God without actually realizing that we are interacting with Him. Saint Paul spoke to the people of Athens about worshiping God unconsciously:

> So Paul, standing in the middle of the Areopagus, said: "Men of Athens, I perceive that in every way you are very religious. For as I passed along, and observed the objects of your worship, I found also an altar with this inscription, 'To an unknown god.' What therefore you worship as unknown, this I proclaim to you. The God, who made the world and everything in it, being Lord of heaven and earth, does not live in shrines made by man, nor is he served by human hands, as though he needed anything, since he himself gives to all men life and breath and everything. And he made from one every nation of men to live on all the face of the earth, having determined allotted periods and the boundaries of their habitation, that they should seek God, in the hope that they might feel after him and find him. Yet he is not far from each one of us, for 'In him we live and move and have our being'..."
>
> (Acts 17:23-28)

The shore is saturated with Christian symbolism. The water of the ocean or lake should remind us of our baptism and how this sacrament initiated our relationship with Christ. Shells, especially the scallop shell, are also associated with the Sacrament of Baptism. Early Christians used these shells to pour water on the heads of those being baptized. The shell is also a symbol of the apostle James the Greater. The symbol of the fish has often been used to represent Jesus Christ. The word "fish" in Greek is "ichthys", which contains the first letters (in Greek) of the phrase "Jesus Christ, Son of God and Savior." People taught that if we lived in the same water as the most noble of all fish, we would live forever with Him. All we need to do is to look for Christ in order for Him to be present.

The omniscient nature of God permits Him to dwell in all things. Christians should use anything possible to link themselves to Jesus. For the beachgoer, the beach is an excellent secular sacramental. It becomes the arena to forge our relationships, to spend time together and love as He ordered us to do. Beach and the rest of nature serves as God's backyard, our place to play, rest and relax while still remaining close to Him. Once the beach or lake becomes a stage where true communion occurs, we have successfully propelled our secular activities towards the spiritual.

The "Footprints Prayer" has become a popular meditation on the intervention of God as we walk through our earthly existence. We often wonder where our Creator is when we strain to find meaning during our struggles. We wonder if He, too, has abandoned us when all others have left us to wander alone. The prayer preaches otherwise:

> One night I had a dream. I was walking along the beach with the Lord, and across the skies flashed scenes from my life. In each scene I noticed two sets of footprints in the sand. One was mine, and one was the Lord's. When the last scene of my life appeared

before me, I looked back at the footprints in the sand, and, to my surprise, I noticed that many times along the path of my life there was only one set of footprints. And I noticed that it was at the lowest and saddest times in my life. I asked the Lord about it: "Lord, you said that once I decided to follow you, you would walk with me all the way. But I notice that during the most troublesome times in my life there is only one set of footprints. I don't understand why you left my side when I needed you most." The Lord said: "My precious child, I never left you during your time of trial. Where you see only one set of footprints, I was carrying you."

The ministry of Jesus began on the shore of the Sea of Galilee. It started with a simple request. After another fruitless night on the water, the Teacher beckoned Peter, Andrew, James and John to set out again onto the lake. The exhausted fishermen had heard it all before. "You should have fished in *this* area and not *that* one!" They were not in the mood to be second-guessed. But Jesus convinced the weary souls to push off onto the lake once again.

The "Footprints" prayer reminds us that Jesus still walks beside us. He desires us to also venture into the deep and unknown. He can transform the commonplace into the extraordinary and make the complex understandable. Jesus aches for our companionship. Why then do we hesitate to get in the boat with Him? Why do we resist joining Him on the journey of a lifetime? This act requires that we place our trust in Him. Our response to the call must be "yes." We may not know what will happen, but with Him beside us, we will not be adrift. We will want for nothing. We need faith and believe that He knows what is best for us even when we feel as if we have seen and done it all before. The Master of the Universe will lead us to ultimate happiness.

As you contemplate life from your beach chair, think how Jesus has summoned you to be one of His disciples. Meditate on how your journey with Him into the unknown will lead you to discover what lies beneath the surface of this world as we make our way to the Kingdom of Heaven. Enjoy your time at the beach or lake and lead others to the "fisher of all men and women." Contemplate how our Savior loved spending time at the shore and how, He too, sought rejuvenation by the water. Include Christ at the beach or lake and experience these places in a whole new way.

ST PAULS

This book was produced by ST PAULS, the publishing house operated by the Society of St. Paul, an international religious congregation of priests and brothers dedicated to serving the Church through the communications media.

For information regarding this and associated ministries of the Pauline Family of Congregations, write to the Vocation Director, Society of St. Paul, 2187 Victory Blvd., Staten Island, New York 10314-6603. Phone us at 718 865-8844.

E-mail: vocation@stpauls.us
www.vocationoffice.org

That the Word of God be everywhere known and loved.